COMMUNITY SECONDARY SCHOOLS IN TANZANIA

COMMUNITY SECONDARY SCHOOLS IN TANZANIA

Challenges and Prospects

by
Elia Shabani Mligo
and
Devotha Lawrence Mshana

Foreword by
Tuli Kassimoto

RESOURCE *Publications* • Eugene, Oregon

COMMUNITY SECONDARY SCHOOLS IN TANZANIA
Challenges and Prospects

Copyright © 2018 Elia Shabani Mligo and Devotha Lawrence Mshana. All rights reserved. Except for brief quotations in critical publications or reviews, no part of this book may be reproduced in any manner without prior written permission from the publisher. Write: Permissions, Wipf and Stock Publishers, 199 W. 8th Ave., Suite 3, Eugene, OR 97401.

Resource Publications
An Imprint of Wipf and Stock Publishers
199 W. 8th Ave., Suite 3
Eugene, OR 97401

www.wipfandstock.com

PAPERBACK ISBN: 978-1-5326-4116-9
HARDCOVER ISBN: 978-1-5326-4117-6
EBOOK ISBN: 978-1-5326-4118-3

Manufactured in the U.S.A.

To Our Beloved Parents,

for their Love and Care of Us from Childhood;

We honor and cherish their great Initiatives

CONTENTS

List of Tables | x
Foreword | xiii
Acknowledgements | xvii
List of Abbreviations and Acronyms | xix

1. INTRODUCTION | 1
    Problem and Objectives
    Significance of the Problem and Study Questions
    Scope and Limitations

2. BACKGROUND STATE OF ACADEMIC PERFORMANCE: THEORETICAL AND EMPIRICAL PERSPECTIVES | 8
    Introduction
    Definitions of Key Terms
    Theoretical Perspectives
    Empirical Perspectives
    Conclusion

3. METHODOLOGICAL PERSPECTIVES | 29
    Introduction
    Scope and Study Design
    Samples and Sampling Procedures
    Instrumentation and Data Processing
    Ethical Considerations
    Conclusion

CONTENTS

4. **CURRENT STATE OF ACADEMIC PERFORMANCE: FINDINGS AND DISCUSSIONS | 37**
   Introduction
   Distribution of Respondents and Used Materials
   i. Questionnaires Return Rate
   ii. Genders and Ages of Respondents
   iii. Academic qualifications of Students, Teachers, and Heads of Schools
   iv. Years of Schools' Establishment
   v. Students' Performance according to Gender
   vi. Years of Experience of Teachers and Heads of Schools
   vii. Sizes of Classrooms and Academic Performance
   viii. General Academic Performance
   ix. Rewards to Students and their Study Habits
   x. Presence of Subject Clubs and Academic Performance

   National Examination Results for Surveyed Community Secondary Schools
   i. Form Four Examination Results Trend for X Secondary School
   ii. Form four Examination Results Trend for Y Secondary School
   iii. Form four Examination Results Trend for Z Secondary school

   Environmental Challenges Influencing Students' Academic Performance
   i. Lack of Adequate Teaching and Learning Facilities
   ii. Poor Learning and Teaching Environment

   The Challenge of Absenteeism and Its Causes: Students' Opinions

CONTENTS

    i.   Punishments and Harsh Treatments

   ii.   Poverty and Sickness

  iii.   Influences from Peer Groups

  iv.   Other Factors causing Absenteeism

Academic Challenges to Teachers and Students

    i.   Shortage of Teaching and Learning Facilities

   ii.   Shortage of Teachers, especially Science Teachers

  iii.   Unfavorable Teaching and Learning Environments

  iv.   Lack of Study Seriousness to Students

   v.   Poor Cooperation among Educational Stakeholders

  vi.   Students' Truant Behavior

 vii.   Other Factors affecting Students' Performance

Conclusion

5.   TOWARDS THE FUTURE OF COMMUNITY SECONDARY SCHOOLS IN TANZANIA | 84

Bibliography | 93

LIST OF TABLES

Table 1: Questionnaires Return Rate | 38
Table 2: Genders and Ages of Respondents | 40
Table 3: Forms which Students Belong | 42
Table 4: Academic Qualifications for Teachers and Heads of Schools | 42
Table 5: Years of Schools' Establishment | 45
Table 6: Academic Performance according to Gender | 45
Table 7: Teachers' Years of Experience | 46
Table 8: Sizes of Classrooms and Students' Academic Performance | 48
Table 9: Does the Number of Students in the Class affect their Academic Performance? | 49
Table 10: General Performance of Form Four National Examinations | 51
Table 11: Do You Provide Rewards to Students who perform Better? | 52
Table 12: Presence of Subject Clubs in Community Secondary Schools | 53
Table 13: Clubs which Students were enrolled | 54
Table 14: X Secondary School Form Four Examination Results Trend (2011—2016) | 55

LIST OF TABLES

Table 15: Y Secondary School Form Four Examination Results Trend (2011—2016) | 56

Table 16: Z Secondary School Form Four Examination Results Trend (2011—2016) | 57

Table 17: Are Facilities to facilitate Learning and Teaching available? | 60

Table 18: Conduciveness of the Environment for Learning | 62

Table 19: Teachers' Findings on the Conduciveness of Environment for Learning | 63

Table 20: Is the Number of Teachers enough and Correspond to the Number of Students? | 72

Table 21: Number of Teachers per Subject | 74

Table 22: Parents' Responses on Educational Issues | 78

Table 23: Is Truancy one of the Problems in Your School? | 80

FOREWORD

SECONDARY EDUCATION IS A pivotal level of education for preparing those who graduate towards entering the work force and preparing excellent ones for tertiary education. Lyimo, Too and Kipng'etich write: "for countries like Tanzania to compete in the global economy, a significant number of citizens need secondary education in order to acquire specific skills and aptitudes necessary for an increasingly technology driven market...."[1] Basing on this stated ambition, since independence in 1961, Tanzania has been struggling to ensure that its citizens acquire adequate education in various fields of study in order to have a literate society. Soon after independence, it was important that Tanzania put clear its educational system in order to acquire political, economic and cultural stability.[2] This was done through the enforcement of establishing secondary schools by government, private and community agencies. Due to this ambition for the government to have a literate society, the government ensured that there was a Community-built secondary school in at least every Ward in the country.

However, the major challenge for these Community-built secondary schools, which now form the majority secondary schools in Tanzania, is based on the academic performance of their students. Students in most of these schools, if not all, have demonstrated low level of critical stance and poor performance in summative examinations prepared by the National Examinations Council of

---

1. Lyimo, Too & Kipng'etich, "Perception of Teachers," 81.
2. Projest, "The Effects of Shortage of Teachers," 1.

xiii

FOREWORD

Tanzania (NECTA).[3] However, Magati, Bosire and Ogeta clearly summarize the main aim of secondary school training which students are supposed to acquire: "While primary education is oriented towards the acquisition of the fundamentals of reading, writing, and mathematics, students at the secondary levels are expected to develop intellectual skills and analyze problems using reasoning and thinking skills, which are inaccessible to younger children."[4] It means that a student is expected to demonstrate distinct abilities from those acquired in the primary level after graduating his/her secondary education studies.

Following the low critical stance and poor performance of students in summative examinations in Community Secondary Schools, contrary to the required expectations stated by Magati, Bosire and Ogeta above, one can ask: Is there any need to have many unmanaged secondary schools, especially Community Secondary Schools, which provide low quality education to the majority citizens who are unfit in the work market within the country and outside? What are the factors causing the law provision of education in the majority Tanzanian Secondary schools, and what initiatives have been taken towards better academic performance in those schools? These and other similar questions are of concern in this book.

Authors of this book, through a research conducted in some secondary schools at Mbeya City in Tanzania argue that the poor academic performance in most Community Secondary Schools in Tanzania is the greatest challenge and need urgent revisit. Several factors have been identified as causative agents of poor performance: those caused by students themselves (e.g., their lack of seriousness and motivation to study hard, their academic procrastination and their absenteeism and truancy), those caused by the respective schools (poor learning environment and lack of adequate facilities), those caused by teachers (lack of adequate experience of school leaders and teachers, harsh languages used by

---

3. Komba, Hizza & Jonathan, "Factors Influencing Academic Performance"; cf. Momanyi, Too & Simiyu, "Effects of Students' Age," 337.

4. Magati, Bosire and Ogeta, "Factors affecting Academic Performance," 3.

FOREWORD

teachers and poor teaching methods employed by teachers when in class), and those caused by parents (poor educational backgrounds of parents and their irresponsibility to countercheck the educational development of their children).[5]

In whatever the case, these results have implications to policy-makers as controllers of the quality of education in Tanzania. The research results presented in this book indicate that despite the good initiatives of the government to enforce the building of Community Secondary Schools in at least every Ward to ensure that children who are eligible to secondary education obtain it, yet it has been reckless in terms of effective monitoring the quality of education provided in these secondary schools. This is clearly indicated by the alarming failures of students in the schools surveyed by the authors of this book. It is important that the question of provision of quality education and quality teaching and learning environment should be in harmony. Hence, it will be less helpful to students entering these schools for the government to concentrate on ensuring sophisticated measuring and evaluating strategies for measuring and evaluating students' academic performance without ensuring the better provision of education required. The measurement and evaluation of students' academic achievements should go hand in hand with the fulfillment of conditions necessary to facilitate the proper fulfillment of planned curricular and syllabuses.[6]

Moreover, the recommendations for future prospects of Community Secondary Schools in this book are clear, directed towards various stakeholders: policy-makers, teachers, heads of respective schools, students and parents. The major problem, as I see it, is not to the research and its findings, which have accomplished their task any way; rather, it is to those to whom the recommendations are directed for action. Will they take heed of the research results discussed in this book, taking trouble to consider

---

5. Komba, Hizza & Jonathan, "Factors Influencing Academic Performance"; Kaguo, "Factors Influencing Academic Performance"; Chonjo, "The Quality of Education"; Clement, "Factors Influencing the Academic Performance."
6. Ogunniyi, *Educational Measurement and Evaluation*.

FOREWORD

and implement for the betterment of the quality of education in the country? How many other research recommendations on this and other related subjects have been made by researchers and have remained in shelves without any consideration for nourishing existing situations? In whatever the case, authors of this book have done their job excellently, despite the humanly weaknesses of their research and presentation of findings. The implications of their findings will be vivid in the reactions of those who read the book. It is my opinion that the Tanzanian secondary educational quality will hardly improve without the educational stakeholders taking heed of the various researches done by experts, including this one, despite the good educational policies the country has. This book is a must read for everybody including policy and decision makers.

Prof. Tuli Kassimoto
Faculty of Education-Teofilo Kisanji University
Mbeya Tanzania

ACKNOWLEDGEMENTS

FIRST, WE WOULD LIKE to thank the Almighty God for providing us strength to accomplish the research and report writing process. Second, a vote of thanks goes to our respondents: headmasters, teachers, Regional and District education administrators, and students of the selected Community Secondary Schools for their cooperation. It is obvious that without them we could hardly have the required data to accomplish our research process

Third, we register special appreciations to our home families: to Mligo's wife Ester and children for their endurance of hardships due to his long absence at home during the whole research period and report writing process; and to Devotha's parents (Dorah Nyambo, Louis Mshana, and Uziah Mshana) for their love, moral, and materials support during the whole research period.

Fourth, this research was done under the auspices of Tumaini University Makumira Mbeya Teaching Centre. We are greatly indebted to this institution for its support through its Research and publication Department. This is because the clearance procedures for this research started by a letter from this University before contacting other higher authorities for permissions. Tumaini University Makumira–Mbeya Teaching Center was an excellent mentor of our research project.

Fifth, this book could not have an attractive appearance it has now without the work of editors and typesetters at Wipf and Stock Publishers. We greatly appreciate for their excellent work. Last, but not least, we appreciate for the cooperation of relatives, friends, fellow lecturers and colleagues who supported us in one way or another during our study period. Thank you very much for making

ACKNOWLEDGEMENTS

this book a reality! We wish them all God's blessings! However, none of the above contributors is responsible for anything presented and discussed in this book. We confess that all shortcomings and strengths of this book fall under our responsibility.

LIST OF ABBREVIATIONS AND ACRONYMS

ACSE	Advanced Certificate of Secondary Education
ACSEE	Advanced Certificate of Secondary Education Examination
c.f.	compare with
e.g.	for example
CSEE	Certificate of Secondary Education Examination
DSEO	District Secondary Education Officer
LoI	Language of Instruction
MOEST	Ministry of Education Science and Technology
n.d.	no date
NECTA	National Examinations Council of Tanzania
NGO	Non-Governmental Organization
p.	page
pp.	pages
SEDP	Secondary Education Development Programme
SPSS	Statistical Package for Social Sciences
TETP	Tanzania Education and Training Policy
UNICEF	United Nations International Children's Emergency Fund
URT	United Republic of Tanzania

Chapter 1

INTRODUCTION

Problem and Objectives

IN THIS CHAPTER WE focus on the introductory matters of this book: background and introduction, statement and significance of the problem, objectives and research questions. In the background of the problem, we explain the role of education, the level of education worldwide, in developed countries and developing countries, in Tanzania as well as the level of education in our study area. Moreover, this chapter describes how this book is important, the problem it addresses and the issues which we mainly concentrate on. Hence, the chapter introduces the importance of education towards development and the way its provision encounters obstacles.

Education plays an important role in the improvement and development of the community and the world at large. It is a right of every human being to acquire it and promotes greatly towards economic development. This is because education helps in eliminating ignorance from people as well as increasing productivity in the country and shaping the behavior of people because people or students will be educated on how to overcome difficulties facing them. Therefore, the contribution of education towards the well-being of humanity indicates the need for the various stakeholders: the family, government and the world at large to put more emphasis on it by creating conducive environments for both teachers and students to have better learning and teaching processes.

As mentioned in the previous paragraph, secondary education plays a vital role in the development of the economy and of people who acquire it. However, according to people's experiences, it shows that the majority of people working in public and private sectors are expected to be secondary education leavers. Moreover, the primary education system relies on teachers who are the product of secondary education system and candidates of higher and tertiary education training are the products of the secondary education system. This is the real meaning of education being the key or the hang pin. Therefore, because of secondary education being important for economic development of any country, of individual citizens, and even of the world at large, there is a need to take measures on the improvement of secondary school environments for learning. This improvement includes preparing conducive environments to both teachers and students, for example laboratories, library and classrooms so as to avoid overcrowding of students in one classroom which can hinder their performance.

The government of the third phase in Tanzania, under President Benjamin William Mkapa, introduced and initiated the implementation of the Tanzania Education and Training Policy (TETP) which led to the increase in students' enrollment from primary schools to secondary schools. The fourth Tanzanian government, beginning from 2006 is one of the main education stakeholders in the country, and is the regime which the policy for Community Secondary Schools was implemented whereby every Ward was supposed to establish a secondary school. This led to increased enrollment of primary school leavers into secondary school education in the country. However, factors affecting academic performance in the initiated Community Secondary Schools are many, and are yet to be studied and reported with adequate intensity.

In developed countries like the United Kingdom and the Unites States of America, the learning process is most advanced; they hardly face challenges as the developing countries do. Instead of the talk about awareness and wastage due to illiteracy of parents,

INTRODUCTION

the developed countries concentrate on funding their education without fear of any wastage. In New York, for example, the government has put up measures to ensure all government secondary schools have most of the required physical facilities like school classrooms and other variables that may lead to effective learning process are intact, and hence maximum students' achievements.[1]

In developing countries, where there are poor physical facilities, governments hardly put more emphasis on the improvement of secondary schools particular preparing conducive learning and teaching environments for students and teachers which would contribute to the better performance. The shortage and poorly constructed classrooms have always been identified as being among the factors that lead to poor performance in both government and private secondary schools. Therefore, this indicates the need for developing countries to put adequate measures to ensure that secondary schools have most of the required physical facilities. Moreover, education to parents on the importance of creating conducive learning environments for their children will greatly help in ensuring better performance in their studies.

Moreover, the educational problems which most developing countries face are the same in Tanzania where the poor performance in Community Secondary Schools is rampant. This makes us ask: what situation that prevail in most Community Secondary Schools in Tanzania in terms of environment for learning, teaching and learning materials, and resources such as laboratories, libraries, enough school classrooms to avoid overcrowding, and effective school administration? What about the question of motivation to students to work hard in their studies in order to lead to effective performance? What about the motivation to teachers in their work places? Do these schools fulfill the purposes of initiating them in terms of the provision of education? Why are there poorer performances in this type of schools than in the other types?

The problem of poor performance in Community Secondary Schools is the situation which has prevailed for a long time in the country and still prevails until now; although these schools

---

1. MOEST, "Report on Sector Review."

struggle to ensure the increase in the performance of their students, yet the problem still prevails. Thus, it is our view that the problem of poor performance is caused by many factors which lead students to hardly concentrating in studying; and this book focuses on analyzing them.

In the area of study, since 1990 when community secondary schools started to operate in Tanzania, there has been an alarming increase in their numbers, whereby in each ward there has been at least one community secondary school initiated by the community. There were about 26 community-built secondary schools and only three (3) government-built secondary schools in the study area by the year 2007.[2] However, in the three selected Community Secondary Schools, poor performance has been the major problem for a number of years until now. Therefore, as stated above, this study concentrates on investigating more on the factors which contribute to students' poor performance at Community Secondary Schools and suggests some measures to be taken so as to improve students' performance. Our main question is this: What are the factors which make most Word secondary schools in Tanzania have poor performance in summative examinations? It is our hypothesis that the poor performance of many Community Secondary Schools in Tanzania, and at the research area in particular, has been associated with different underlying problems such as poor socio-cultural, socioeconomic, school environment, socio-political factors, lack of family support as well as shortage of different learning and teaching materials and resources.

Mostly, students in Community Secondary Schools experience poor performance. According to URT, poor academic performance in most community secondary schools in the country has been a major concern by the government; and it is this problem which this study deals with. The government has argued on the quality of secondary education in Tanzania that it remains a concern with the percentage of students passing the form IV

---

2. Mbeya Regional Education Office, Personal Communication, June 2017.

INTRODUCTION

examination showing that there is only a slight improvement from 33.5 percent in 2006 to 35.7 percent in 2007.[3]

The Tanzanian government introduced secondary education program (SEDP) for the expansion and improvement of government and community-built secondary schools. Many researchers have tried to study about this problem of poor performance, for instance Lam who investigated the community secondary schools phenomena and the perpetuation of inequality in performance.[4] Omari also examined the widespread community and government built schools in Tanzania and their poor performance,[5] and Boma assessed the factors influencing good performance in Tanzanian secondary schools.[6] Therefore, these surveys indicate that due to poor performance of students in Community Secondary Schools, the major purpose for introducing such schools has been well articulated in terms of students' enrolment for secondary education, but hardly in terms of the required academic performance.

Significance of the Problem and Study Questions

As stated in the above paragraphs, this study investigated the factors that contribute to students' poor performance in Community Secondary Schools in Tanzania and in the study area in particular. Most Community Secondary Schools are considered to be schools which students have poor performance in their studies; teachers and students themselves are required to seek for plausible answers why students are not successful at their exams with a goal to raise exam scores and continuously search for ways to maintain exam scores. If schools can determine what factors hinder students' achievements, they can begin creating and employing different strategies that assist in students' achievements.

3. URT, "Poverty and Human Development."
4. Lam, *Generating Extreme Inequality*.
5. Omari, "Education in Tanzania."
6. Boma, "Factors affecting Performance."

One significance of the problem studied emanate from the data collected. The data collected from this study help in providing Community Secondary Schools authorities at the study area and to the country as a whole to address the significant factors that contribute to students' poor performance. For them, the data provide guidelines to take an action of implementing educational innovations and interventions in order to directly address those factors within their own campuses and abandon future hindrances. Moreover, this study suggests some possible remedies to be taken in order to deal with the situation of poor performance in Community Secondary Schools. Hence, it will be helpful to curriculum developers and implementers to guide them in identifying which areas to put more emphasis on in order to improve performance of both science and art subjects in Secondary Schools.

Limitation of the Study

Having discussed the significance of the problem in the previous section, this paragraph highlights some limitations. Limitations are obstacles or conditions beyond the ability of the researcher that may hinder him or her from having desirable conclusions of the study and the application of those conclusions to other situations. In other words, limitations are constraints which the researcher faces in the execution of the study. This study was constrained by the following aspects:

i. Delay in obtaining the permission for research from relevant authorities in the research clearance stage for us to collect data in the selected schools. Despite the late permission, we were able to collect adequate data to accomplish our research purpose.

ii. Inadequate funds to cover a large sample in the whole area as the topic suggests. To make the research feasible, three Community Secondary Schools were selected to represent the rest of schools in the selected population.

INTRODUCTION

iii. Some of the respondents (especially students) were reluctant to provide information during the study, most likely due to fear of being victimized by their teachers and fellows, and some teachers had limited time because of their duties like marking exams. We assured students of high confidentiality and anonymity of their names in the report, and teachers were consulted by appointments in the times they were at easy.

Chapter 2

BACKGROUND OF ACADEMIC PERFORMANCE

Theoretical and Empirical Perspectives

Introduction

THE PREVIOUS CHAPTER INTRODUCED the problem and its significance; this chapter deals with the previous theoretical and empirical studies on the issue of academic performance. Addressing issues theoretically and empirically involves reviewing literatures. Literature review involves reading the works of other researchers who have dealt with the problem which you intend to deal with, or which are similar to yours.[1] According to Neuman, literature review is important in any study because of the following aspects: first, it helps the researcher to know what is already known about the problem stated (the current state of knowledge about the issues being studied); whether there is somebody who has done a study exactly the same or similar to the one which the researcher intends to do as well as knowing the gap of research which needs to be filled. Second, it helps the researcher to narrow down his or her research problem. Other researchers studied particular

---

1. Mligo, *Introduction to Research*, 66.

problems in particular contexts. Their studies help the researcher to see how they narrowed their problems, which eventually lead the researcher to narrowing his or her own. Third, it stimulates the researcher's creativity and curiosity in the process of research. Literature review is a stimulating agent to the researcher because, through reading and making sense of other people's researches, the researcher finds his or her own way different from what others have just passed through. Fourth, the researches of others are models of the way the researcher should write his or her own research report. In this case, the researcher builds on past researches in order to construct his or her own. Past researches form the basis of the research being done.[2]

Aiming at contextualizing the research into previous researches, literature review may concentrate into a particular theory or theories which are relevant to the study being done, into particular previous empirical researches done, or into both of them.[3] This chapter forms the background part of our study. It concentrates on the literature review which defines important terminologies frequently used in the study, discusses appropriate theories for basing the study, provides an empirical framework which surveys the various past studies conducted in regard to challenges facing Community Secondary Schools, and indicates the gap covered in this study. In dealing with the mentioned aspects, the chapter lays down a foundation for the collection and analysis of the study findings.

Definition of Key Terms

Every study has its own terminologies which are frequently repeated or which hold the main argument of that study. These terms need to be defined and clarified for readers to clearly follow the argument of the respective study report. The key terms and concepts defined in this section are the following: student, academic

---

2. Neuman, *Basics of Social Research*, 69.
3. Paltridge & Starfield, *Thesis and Dissertation Writing*, 99.

performance, and Community Secondary Schools. Hence, the definitions of these terms will remove the possible ambiguity to readers to navigate across the book as they are frequently used in the whole study.

According to *Merriam Webster Dictionary*, a student is a person enrolled and attends school, college, or University pursuing a particular kind of study. Students are the ones considered unknowledgeable about a particular field and are to be equipped with knowledge and skills. Students play an important role to ensure better school performance in different activities by studying hard and concentrating much in their studies and what their teachers teach them for the aim of ensuring better performance. Therefore, being a student is a stage in ones process of being a knowledgeable person in a particular stage of study. Being a student in secondary schools is the third stage in one's educational process.

There are three stages in the Tanzanian educational system. The first stage, according to the Tanzanian educational system, is the kindergarten or pre-primary education and primary education; and the second stage is secondary education. Secondary education is further subdivided into two: ordinary level secondary education (form I–IV) which leads the student to acquiring a CSE and advanced level secondary education (form V–VI) which leads to acquiring an ACSE. The third stage is tertiary education which comprises of college and university education. Therefore, a student requires performing well in order to transcend from one stage to the other in the academic ladder.

As just stated in the previous paragraph, being a student involves acquiring a particular competence in what one studies. Acquiring competence is measured by the way that student performs. What then is performance and how is it measured? Merriam Webster defines performance as the fulfillment of a claim, promise or request. Moreover, Adediwura and Tayo define academic performance as the display of knowledge attained or skills developed in school subjects designated by test and examination scores or marks assigned by the subjects' teachers.[4] Unity and Igbudu further

---

4. Adediwura & Tayo, "Perception of Teachers' Knowledge."

BACKGROUND OF ACADEMIC PERFORMANCE

define academic performance thus: "Academic achievement is the outcome of education, that is, the extent which a student, teacher or institution has achieved their educational goals. Academic achievement is commonly measured by examination or continuous assessment but there is no general agreement on how it is best tested or which aspect is most important knowledge such as facts . . . ."[5] Moreover, Bell explains that academic performance is described at the state level as an evaluation of students' performance on standardized tests geared towards specific ages and based on a set of achievements students in each age group are expected to meet.[6] Following the above definitions of adequate academic performance, poor performance in Community Secondary Schools is defined as a performance that the examinee considers as falling below an expected standard of a particular set measurement.

In Tanzania, academic performance is measured by indicators such as "marks scored, grades and divisions obtained by candidates with respect to the examination standard board of a country such as National Examination Council of Tanzania (NECTA)."[7] David succinctly describes the performance measurements done by NECTA in the CSE thus: "The NECTA criteria of awarding divisions is as follows: A candidate who sits for NECTA examinations is awarded divisions I, II, III, IV or 0 on meeting the following conditions: Division One (I); passes in at least 7 subjects passes at grade A or B or C in at least five subjects. Reaches an aggregate of more than or 11 equal to 7 points but less than or equal to 17 points, taking the best seven subjects . . . . Division Two (II): Passes in at least 7 subjects, passes at grade A or B or C in at least four subjects and reaches an aggregate of more than or equal to 18 points but less than or equal to 21 points, taking the candidates' best seven subjects. Division Three (III); passes in at least seven subjects one of which must be at grade A or B or C or

---

5. Unity & Igbudu, "Influence of Gender", 102.

6. Bell, "Definition of Academic Performance," cf. Njabili, *Public Examinations*, 57–71; Ogunniyi, *Educational Measurement*, 6–39.

7. David, "Determinants of Poor Academic Performance," 10–11; cf. Nakalema & Ssenyonga, "Academic Stress," 8

passes in at least five subjects two of which must be at grade A or B or C. Reaches an aggregate of more than or equal to 22 points but less than or equal to 25 points, taking the candidates' best seven subjects. Division Four (IV): Passes in at least one subject at grade A, B or C, or passes in two subjects at grade D, reaches an aggregate of more than or equal to 26 points to 33 points but less than or equal to 33 points, taking the candidate's best seven subjects. Division Zero (O): does not fulfill the conditions for awards of the divisions (I-IV) . . . ."[8] These stated measures are done after the student performs the Certificate of Secondary Education Examinations (CSEE) conducted by the NECTA.

As exemplified in the title of this book, the study concerns schools located in Wards.[9] According to the *Oxford Advanced Learner's Dictionary* of 2006, the term "ward" means one of the areas into which a city is divided and which is presented by member of the local council. In this book, "a ward refers to a subdivision of a municipality." The term "*secondary school*" as we use in this book refers to the level of study above primary school and below tertiary education which is offered in colleges and universities. And, the term 'Community Secondary Schools' is used to refer to those secondary schools constructed and established by communities within these localities, and which the government is responsible for distributing teaching and learning materials. In this sense, they are known as government schools. The schools were introduced in the third phase of the Tanzanian government in order to meet the need to increase the number of students' enrolment in secondary schools. In this case, Community Secondary Schools, being built

8. David, "Determinants of Poor Academic Performance," 11.

9. There are two main categories of secondary schools currently existing in Tanzania: first, Government and private secondary schools. Government secondary schools are further divided into two: the traditional national secondary schools whole construction is originally governmental, and community built secondary schools whose construction is originally by community initiatives but handed to the government to manage. The second category is private secondary schools which are built and owned by individuals and NGO's and communities, e.g., Seminaries (cf. David, "Determinants of Poor Academic Performance," 2014: 9-10)

BACKGROUND OF ACADEMIC PERFORMANCE

by community members, provide chances for students who are qualified to be enrolled into secondary schools but do not have chances to be enrolled into purely government built secondary schools.[10]

Theoretical Perspectives

The theoretical perspective in the literature review is concerned with the theories which link between the theoretical aspects and practical components of the investigation undertaken. The argument in this book is guided by two theories that explain why there is a relationship between students' performance and the learning process in Community Secondary Schools studied: the theory of organization, and the motivation theory. We discuss each of these theoretical perspectives below.

General Systems Theory of Organization

Social units of people who are managed and function together in order to achieve a certain intended goal constitute an organization. Ludwig Von Bertalanffy (1901—1972), an Australian biologist advocated the General Systems Theory which contends that all parts of an organization are interrelated such that changing one part of the system in an organization affects other parts as well. This theory is based on Aristotle's statement: "The whole is more than the sum of its parts...."[11]

Earlier in his life (ca. 1920s), Bertalanffy wrote: "Since the fundamental character of the living thing is its organization, the customary investigation of the single parts and processes cannot provide a complete explanation of the vital phenomena. This investigation gives us no information about the coordination of

---

10. See Komba, Hizza & Jonathan, "Factors influencing Academic Performance"; Kaguo, Factors influencing Academic Performance," 3; David, "Determinants of Academic Performance," 10.

11. Bertalanffy, "The History and Status," 407.

parts and processes. Thus the chief task of biology must be to discover the laws of biological systems (at all levels of organization). We believe that the attempts to find a foundation for theoretical biology points at a fundamental change in the world picture. This view, considered as a method of investigation, we shall call "*organismic biology*" and, as an attempt at an explanation, "*the system theory of the organism.*"[12] These words indicate that the theory is not only limited to biological sciences, but also other spheres of organization by replacing the word "organism" with the referred organization. Hence, according to this theory, a school is an organism, an organization which needs order of its parts in order to constitute the whole.

The General Systems Theory was first pronounced by Bertalanffy in the year 1030 when he wrote: "There exist models, principles and laws that apply to generalized systems or their subclasses irrespective of their kind, the nature of their component elements, and the relations or 'forces' between them. We postulate a new discipline called General System Theory." In this case, as Bertalanffy says in his own words, the "General Systems Theory, then consists of the scientific exploration of 'wholes' or 'wholeness'...."[13]

According to the General Systems Theory, School organizations are complex social systems whose properties cannot be known from analysis of the constituent elements in isolation. For effective management of the teaching-learning process, emphasis should shift from parts to the whole. As applied to this study, this theory will be helpful to emphasize that organizations of Schools are most important to ensure better performance of students in Schools whereby all units are required to work together by having great relationship from all systems. Thus, the performance of a system depends on how the elements work together and not how each element works independently; and for the effective learning

---

12. Bertalanffy, "The History and Status," 410, cf. Bertalanffy, *General Systems Theory*, 30–36; Helou & Caddy, "Definition Problems," 79–80.

13. Bertalanffy, "The History and Status," 415, cf. Bertalanffy, *General Systems Theory*, 30–36; Helou & Caddy, "Definition Problems," 79–80.

BACKGROUND OF ACADEMIC PERFORMANCE

process and better output in a School organization system the input factor which is available in a School should be well managed. However, this theory has its strengths and weaknesses. The strength of General Systems Theory of organizations is that it puts more emphasis on the importance of the parts or sections of the organization to work together and not working independently which helps in directing and governing accountability of any part of the organization and in directing the systematic performance of work. The weakness of this theory, according to our view, is that it hardly explains clearly how these parts will work together to ensure better performance of a particular organization.

As applied to this study the General Systems Theory of organizations will be helpful as the way of advocating all heads of schools, heads of departments, as well as teachers to work together to fulfill their responsibilities and duties as they require to do transparently with greater accountability to ensure better performance in their respective schools, especially in Community Secondary Schools. This theoretical perspective is selected because organization is important in any institution to ensure a better success of that institution; all parts of the institution are required to be well organized and work together for the fulfillment of the institution's goal. Therefore, for students to achieve better performance in their schools there should be better organization by ensuring that all parts of the school work together towards the whole.

Motivation Theory

In his theory of motivation, Abraham Maslow (1908—1970), an American psychologist, proposes an intrinsic motivation which comes from within the student or from factors inherent in the task being performed. On the one hand, according to Baranek, "intrinsic motivation is the act of completing an activity for the pleasure of doing the activity itself. Extrinsic motivation, on the other hand, is the act of completing an activity in order to receive some type of reward from another source."[14] For example, students who love to read are intrinsically motivated to read; there is something about reading that they enjoy and that makes them want to do it even if there is no reward for it from outside.

For the aim of promoting intrinsic motivation some strategies may be used including arousing interest in the subject matter, maintaining curiosity, using a variety of interesting presentation modes, and helping students set their own goals. A number of other strategies such as student choice, demonstrating the relevance or usefulness of content, and collaboration can also help encourage intrinsic motivation. As applied to this study encouraging intrinsic motivation to students through the use of these strategies may help to increase performance to students because motivating them encourages reading more for students to attain better performance. Moreover, teachers are also required to be motivated so that they can increase efforts in the teaching process; hence, a better performance to their students.

The strength of motivation theory is that it explains the way in which intrinsic motivation is important to ensure students' performance for various motivation strategies to be employed that can encourage students to read more for those who love to read. The weakness of this theory is that it becomes slow to change the behavior of those who do not love to read; it also requires long preparation and special attention, especially to slow learners who cannot easily be motivated.

However, this theory is applied to our study in discussing the factors which contribute to the poor performance at Community Secondary Schools in Tanzania, especially at Uyole-Village Mbeya where this study was conducted. Maslow's Motivation theory will be helpful, where teachers are required to motivate their students according to their performance in different studies, which will help to encourage all students who do not love to read for them to read more because teachers will ensure students' inner motivation and an urge to read in order for them to pass their examinations. This means that it will help students to increase school performance

14. Baranek, "The effect of Rewards," 5.

BACKGROUND OF ACADEMIC PERFORMANCE

especially in Community Secondary Schools through the intrinsic motivation enhanced to them. Moreover, this theoretical perspective is selected because motivation is one of the factors which can encourage students to study hard to ensure better performance.

As introduced above, this type of motivation is not the one obtained by external incentives as purported by the theory of operant conditioning developed by Skinner (1948). Skinner's theory "works on the premise that if a reinforcer is delivered after a certain behavior is performed, then the strength of the behavior is increased...."[15] For example, motivating students by giving them some rewards, positive reward for those students who perform well in their subjects and negative reward (punishment) for those who do not perform well can also be used as means of encouraging students to study hard; hence, enhancing better performance. Hence, intrinsic motivation arouses students inner self-urge to learn whereby the student oneself sees the need to study hard without being pushed by external rewards.

Empirical Perspectives

Having discussed the two theories which guide the argument of this book, this part reviews some literatures which have dealt with the issue of performance in secondary schools. Empirical literature review involves searching for the real things from the empirical situations; it is searching for what other scholars have found, those who went to the field directly.[16] According to Msabila and Nalaila, empirical literature review is based on those who collected data from primary sources of information that were obtained through actual observations by another person in the form of research or through witnessing the occurrence.[17] Therefore, these empirical literature reviews help us to know what others have done in relation to our study and what they have not done, which help us fill

---

15. Baranek, "The effect of Rewards," 11.
16. Mligo, *Introduction to Research*.
17. Msabila & Nalaila, *Research Proposal*, 68.

the gap of what they have not done. The review of literatures in this part is based on the following themes: the question of education and development, methods of instruction, the way of assessing and evaluating students, and the availability of teaching and learning materials.

Education and Development

We start our review of empirical literatures by exploring the theme of education and development. The URT speaking on education and development says that there is a positive relationship between education and development; and this relationship depends mainly on the extent to which the kind of education provided and its methods are capable of meeting the expectations of the individuals who acquire it and the needs of society to which the individual joins after acquiring such education. In this understanding, education and its guiding philosophy refers to development efforts made by the Tanzanian government towards achieving a self-reliance education for her people.[18] The URT advocates that a "Good system of education in any country must be effective on two fronts: on the *quantitative* level, to ensure access to education and equity as well as allocation of resources to various segments of the society, and on the *qualitative* level to ensure that the country produces the skills needed for rapid social and economic development. Evidence exists to show a very high correlation between investment in education and the creation of the national wealth."[19]

The strength of the above notion by the URT is that it helps in explaining the relationship between education and development, whereby education to people is the one thing which leads to social and economic development in the country, which further means that education plays an important role towards development. However, the weakness of this notion is that it hardly explains how education should be provided to people so as to ensure

---

18. URT, *Tanzania Education and Training Policy*.
19. Ibid., v.

BACKGROUND OF ACADEMIC PERFORMANCE

country development as well, as in which way education should be provided. Therefore, despite its weakness ideas from this notion help us to assess if there is any relationship between development and education by looking at school achievements which depend on students' performance and their contribution to development issues.

Methods of Instructions

The second theme concerns methods of instructions used in teaching and learning process. Methods of instructions contribute greatly in the success or failure in academic performance in schools. Mosha did research about methods of instruction whereby he found out that teaching methods related to students' achievements, and therefore proper instructional methods used in schools leads to good academic performance. The methods of instruction involve the way teachers use to present materials to students such as various techniques as well as the use of language to present materials to students.[20] As Mosha has just found out, the method of instruction contributes much to the increase or decrease in the students' performance.

Mosha's investigation on the method of instructions is very important in that it tries to explain about the importance of methods of teaching that teachers should use in order to ensure that their students perform well in examinations, such as the way teachers should present materials to their students. The other strength of Mosha's study is that it explains about the importance of the language used to present the materials to students. However, the weakness of Mosha's investigation on the methods of instructions is that it hardly explains how teachers can collect feedbacks as to whether students understand or not, and how students respond to a particular method of teaching.

However, as applied to our study, Mosha's study is useful because it helps us to assess whether methods of instructions in

20. Mosha, "Primary Education."

schools which our research was conducted are applicable or not. And if not, this will be on our initial report side as a recommendation to teachers on the importance of applying appropriate methods of instructions during teaching so as to make students understand their teaching well, hence assuring better academic performance.

Students' Assessment and Evaluation

The third theme explored students' assessment and evaluation in regard to their academic competence. The ultimate act of the process of teaching students is evaluating the competence gained by such students in what was taught. The assessment and evaluation of students' performance has to be effectively done. Ndalichako studied the process of classroom students' formative assessment and evaluation through observations of students in the process of learning, the collection of frequent feedback on students' learning, and the design of modest classroom experiments. She also investigated the support which school authorities provide to teachers in their evaluation process. A questionnaire was distributed to teachers who marked the Certificate of Secondary Education Examinations in 2013 in order to accomplish her study. She found that teachers could learn much about how students learn, and more specifically, how students respond to particular teaching approaches. However, it was discovered that most teachers used traditional methods in assessing and evaluating students' study activities. The heavy teaching workloads to teachers greatly hindered their effective evaluation and assessment processes; hence, failing to obtain comprehensive pictures of the way students learned in their classrooms. The predominant support which school authorities provided to teachers was that of providing the needed materials to conduct the assessment which, to some extent, was not enough to make their work more effective.[21]

---

21. Ndalichako, "Examining Classroom Assessment Practice," cf., Ndalichako, "Towards an Understanding of Assessment."

BACKGROUND OF ACADEMIC PERFORMANCE

Assessment and evaluation of student's performance is important in ensuring the students' continuity in their studies. We agree with Ndalichako that "What is assessed and how assessment is done play a significant role in determining the effectiveness of teaching and learning." As advocated by Ndalichako's study, students' assessment and evaluation helps teachers to understand whether their students understand or not. Moreover, Ndalichako's study explains clearly the ways of doing assessment and evaluation. Some ways she mentions are the use of portfolios and projects, despite the normal timed tests. The study is highly illuminating because it exemplifies the ways and procedures of evaluating students. However, this perspective is useful to our book because it helps us to assess whether there is availability of teaching and learning materials in schools where we conducted research, and whether teachers use a variety of assessment methods to ascertain students' performance development. Moreover, it will enable us provide recommendations to address the importance of having enough teaching and learning materials and using a variety of assessment methods and resources to ensure better student's performance instead of depending on only one method.

Availability of Learning and Teaching Materials and Resources

The forth theme we explored concerned the availability of learning and teaching materials for both students and teachers. Despite the proper and effective evaluation, done by using effective evaluation methods, teaching and learning materials are necessary in schools to enhance better teaching and learning processes. A better and effective evaluation will be possible if a better teaching and learning environment is applied. Chonjo researched on the availability of learning and teaching materials and resources. He found out that insufficient teaching materials and poor methods of teaching were factors that led to poor performance of Secondary Schools in Tanzania. The availability of teaching and learning materials such as textbooks, teacher's guides, reference books, classroom charts, maps, chemicals and laboratory apparatuses are important in ensuring students' performance; thus, they can help to make students' learning processes easy because materials are accessible. Moreover, the availability of teaching and learning resources such as school classrooms, libraries, laboratories, toilets, dormitories, desks, tables, and chairs were some of the important things to be considered to ensure the better performance to the students according to Chonjo's study.[22]

In this study, Chonjo also found that the availability of well-trained teachers was not in place in most Tanzanian primary schools. Chonjo wrote thus in the 1994s:

> A considerable number of primary school teachers are primary school leavers themselves who have attended teacher training course for a period not exceeding two years. Some of these have been trained through a residential training programme, while others went through what is called Distant Teacher Training Programme. These teachers have a low level of education, and are expected to teach any subject in the primary school curriculum. Many of these teachers are handicapped in terms of the level of awareness, experience and academic rigor. The Ministry has constantly made efforts to upgrade this group of teachers through in-service programmes, but the problem is still far from being solved.[23]

More than two decades have passed since Chonjo reported the above findings. The question is whether the situation has changed. It is possible that few aspects have changed; however, most of the aspects remain far from being changed.

One of the strengths of Chonjo's research on the availability of learning and teaching materials and resources is its emphasis on the importance of the availability of teaching and learning materials and resources to increase students' performance in their studies. However, Chonjo's study does not explain which type of materials

22. Chonjo, "The Quality of Education," cf., Lyimo, Too & Kipng'etich, "Perception of Teachers"; Elibariki, "Factors influencing Shortage of Teaching-Learning Resources.

23. Chonjo, "The Quality of Education," 43.

and resources are important in supporting student's performance. Chonjo's study would be more important if it analyzed teaching and learning materials in terms of their utmost importance, and materials which each school should make sure to have them despite its economic situation. This analysis is important because, for Community Secondary Schools, it is hardly possible to have all materials required materials in the teaching and learning process.

Teachers' Experiences, Learning Environments and Subject Clubs

The fifth theme is about the contribution of experiences of teachers, the learning environments and the presence of subject clubs to academic performance. The experience of teachers in their teaching career, the environment to which students are subjected during their study time and the existence of subject clubs at schools are some among the crucial factors which determine the students' performance in their summative examinations. Nyangosia conducted research to determine the differential Kenya certificate of Secondary school education performance. The study was done at Nyeri and Kiambu in the Republic of Kenya. Nyangosia found that the following factors were evident: low work experiences of teachers and heads of schools, most of them had stayed at their respective schools for less than five years. Despite the low experiences of teachers and heads of schools, there were various strategies employed to improve performance. Some of them were instructional strategies (e.g., updating professional documents providing all the needed teaching and learning materials, holding regular staff meetings to discuss challenges and prospects, involving teachers in the decisions of issues regarding the best strategies to improve teaching, better supervision of teachers to complete their syllabuses within the allocated time, ensuring a better teamwork exists, having regular staff performance appraisals, and heads visiting teachers in classes when they teach in order to supervise their teaching).[24]

Despite the instructional strategies, there were those strategies which related to school safety and orderliness, such as ensuring the school climate was conducive for teaching and learning, ensuring orderliness and cleanliness of the school compound, effective guidance and counseling to students, better cooperation with parents in discussing about students' disciplines, teachers' involvement in discerning the better ways to improve discipline, and ensuring that the schools have most of the necessary material resources for teaching and learning. Another strategy was the clarification of the mission and vision of the respective school, such as reminding students to stick to their core function as students throughout their student life, monitoring teachers to work towards the school's goal, motivating teachers and students to stick to the set goals for each subject taught. Strategies relating to home-school relation included reminding parents on their duty when students were at home, having regular meetings with parents to discuss students trends in academic performance, reminding parents on the way they should ensure conducive home environments for their children to study comfortably including their provision of support spiritually, morally and materially. Other strategies were those relating to monitoring students; academic progress. These included regular assessments by tests and assignments, and having regular academic meetings to discuss students' academic progresses, and discussing academic progress with individual students. These strategies enhanced better performance despite the low experiences of teachers and heads of schools.[25]

Nyangosia's study is highly illuminating because it puts clear all the necessary strategies which were used to ensure performance, and which can be adopted by any other school in the African context towards academic progress. Moreover, it shows that teachers experience in teaching alone can hardly work effectively without considering other school environmental factors relating to

24. Nyangosia, "Determinants of Differential Kenya Certificate."
25. Ibid.

BACKGROUND OF ACADEMIC PERFORMANCE

students, teachers and school campus. However, this study hardly discusses the weaknesses which schools at Nyeri and Kiambu had. This lack of discussion indicates that the study neglected the other side of the coin (the negative part) in the midst of the successes of schools due to workable strategies set. The study could be even more illuminating and insightful if it balanced its discussion by including the weak points which the schools had. Balancing the discussion is important because the coin always has two sides.

Another study was conducted by Lugayila in Maswa District in the United Republic of Tanzania. The study examined the determinants of poor performance in examinations among secondary school students within the district. Using Maslow's theory of motivation as his theoretical perspective and interview as a method of collecting data, Lugayila found out that some factors affecting students' performance in examinations were: learning environments, lack of students' readiness to study hard in order to achieve better examination results, distance from home to schools which encouraged truancy and absenteeism, inadequate teachers' and students' intrinsic motivation, poor teaching and learning methods, improper student-desks ratio, improper students-books ratio, teachers' inability to properly use the allocated time in the timetables, and poor accessibility of the library and library services.[26]

Moreover, Kaguo conducted a study to determine the factors influencing students' academic performance to secondary schools in Mbeya Region Tanzania. His main focus was on both government and community built secondary schools. In the schools he selected for survey, Kaguo found out that there were enough teaching materials in government built secondary schools and poor in most community built secondary schools. Community built secondary schools indicated lack of required exercises provided to students while government built secondary schools were far better. Moreover, both government and community built secondary schools showed having a language barrier in studying the taught subject contents. Language hindered their understanding

---

26. Lugayila, "Assessment of Factors," cf., Mhonjiwa, "Factors influencing Poor Examination Performance."

of what was taught in classes.²⁷ This issue will be discussed in the following subheading.

However, both types of schools indicated the existence of subject clubs in their schools which enhanced better practice of both the language and the subjects concerned. The lack of lunch at school, for both types of schools caused the increase in truancy and absenteeism of students, which in turn caused poor performance in examinations. Financial problems of parents and distance from home to school were also among the factors which made students' minds unsettled, hence affecting their concentration in studies. After comparing the two types of schools in terms of the above listed aspects, Kaguo concluded that being a government or community-built secondary school did not matter if the necessary conditions were supplied to students. In his study, community-built secondary schools had poorer performance as compared to government-built secondary schools due to lack of most necessary requirements to enhance better performance.²⁸

Language of Instruction

The sixth theme was about the language used in the teaching and learning process. The language of instruction issue pointed out by Kaguo's study in the above paragraphs has been of great discussion in Tanzania. Some scholars have been in support that English, the language currently used for instruction in secondary schools should continue being used,²⁹ while others reject that English language should be replaced with Kiswahili, the most spoken language in the Tanzanian context.³⁰ The main argument of

27. Kaguo, "Factors influencing Academic Performance."
28. Ibid., cf. Komba, Hizza & Jonathan, "Factors influencing Academic Performance"; Mkalangale, "The Poor Performance of Students."
29. E.g., Nyamubi, "Students' Attitudes."
30. E.g., Qorro, "Language of Instruction in Tanzania"; Qorro, "Language of Instruction and Its Effects"; Qorro, "Does Language of Instruction affect Quality?" Qorro, "Matatitizo ya Kutumia Kiingereza" ; Neke, "English in Tanzania"; Neke, "The Medium of Instruction in Tanzania"; Lupogo, "The

BACKGROUND OF ACADEMIC PERFORMANCE

those who support the use of English is that it is an international language prominent in Business and international relations, while those who reject its continual use argue that English is the representative of the hegemonic culture of the colonizers (Britain). The consensus on which language is appropriate as a language of instruction in Tanzania has not been reached yet. Currently, English is used as a language of instruction in minority English-Medium pre-primary schools and English-Medium primary schools, and all secondary schools, colleges and Universities. And Kiswahili is used as a language of instruction to the majority pre-primary and primary schools. However, the majority of the above researches, especially those who do not support the use of English as a language of instruction, indicate that students fail to perform well in study processes and examinations due to the language barrier. English language is foreign to Tanzanian people, a language not spoken in the everyday life of majority Tanzanians. Hence, most students are unable to use it because of not being well-equipped with it from pre-primary and primary schools.

Conclusion

In the above discussion, we have not been exhaustive to discuss all factors which make students have poor performance. It is real that there are many factors which influence students in their process of study leading them to poor or better performance including methods of instructions, the language used in teaching, students' assessment and evaluation, the availability of teaching and learning materials and resources, teachers' and students' altitudes or perceptions on education, sources of school funds, distances to school, and teaching and learning environments All these and other similar factors contribute to better or poor student's performance.

In spite of the above studies elaborating on some of the factors contributing to poor performance in Community Secondary

---

Intensity of Language of Instruction"; Brock-Utne & Desai, "Expressing Oneself" and Brock-Utne & Holmersdotir, "Language Policies."

Schools, they hardly discussed the prospects of the schools where studies were done. Since every situation has two sides of the coin, it is important to look at both sides of the coin in order to ascertain the whole reality. Therefore, our study aims at investing the challenges which contribute to students' poor performance especially in Community Secondary Schools in Tanzania and the prospects of those schools despite their existing challenges. Following the research results, more challenges which contribute to poor performance in Community Secondary Schools are discussed in detail such as parents' supports on educational issues, students' behavior to their teachers as well as motivation to both teachers and students, which are also important factors for encouraging students to concentrate much in their studies.

Chapter 3

METHODOLOGICAL PERSPECTIVES

Introduction

AFTER REVIEWING THE LITERATURES in the previous chapter, this chapter discusses the methodology of the study. Methodology, according to Msabila and Nalaila, is a systematic study of methods that are, can be, or have been applied within a discipline.[1] According to Mligo, methodology is a global style of thinking and a general approach to studying research topics. It is an overall research strategy.[2] One main assumption of a well-presented methodology is that it can enable other researchers to replicate the study using the same presented methodology.[3] Our methodological perspective in this chapter follows the above-presented aspects. It discusses the scope of the study, research design, samples, sample size and sampling procedures, research instruments, data analysis, data reporting and ethical issue considered, this is because these research methodologies directed us which instruments, type of design that was needed to be followed in order to conduct the study properly.

1. Msabila & Nalaila, *Research Proposal*.
2. Mligo, *Introduction to Research*.
3. Paltridge & Starfield, *Thesis and Dissertation Writing*, 114.

COMMUNITY SECONDARY SCHOOLS IN TANZANIA

Scope and Study Design

We begin this chapter by discussing the scope of our study. The scope of the study discusses the parameters into which a particular study is conducted. Our study was carried out in Mbeya City Council, Tanzania whereby three Community Secondary Schools were involved in the study. These schools ware Itezi, Uyole and Pankumbi Community Secondary Schools. Data were collected from respondents of three categories which are students, teachers, and Headmasters. This study was done at Uyole-Village which is at Mbeya City Council area because of easy availability of resources and the Schools in this area are close to one another; hence, it was easier to travel from one school area to another without any hardship; and also it was because we were familiar with this place and the problem of poor performance that prevailed much in Community Secondary Schools found in Uyole-Village. In this case, we found that the three selected schools could be good representatives of other Community Secondary Schools in the country.

An effective conventional research comprises a well-decided research design. Mouton and Marais write thus about research and research process: "the research process is essentially a decision-making process in which the researcher is continuously involved, among other things, in making decisions about what ought to be investigated and how this ought to be done."[4] These words mean that research is not something out there. Rather, it is something the researcher decides, designs, and executes. It is like building a house. The house is not something outside there; rather, it is something that is decided, designed, and executed. Therefore, as the builder of a house designs it before erecting, with his or her own decision on how it should be, it is so to any effective research.

What then is research design? According to Mouton and Marais, "*A research design is the arrangement of conditions for collection and analysis of data in a manner that aims to combine relevance to the research purpose with economy in procedure . . . .*"[5]

---

4. Mouton and Marais, *Basic Concepts*, 29.
5. Ibid., 32.

METHODOLOGICAL PERSPECTIVES

This study adopted a *case study* design which involves both qualitative and quantitative approaches. In this case study Mbeya City and the Community Secondary Schools in it was the unit of our detailed study whereby various trends of performance in selected Community Secondary Schools were examined.[6] However, the quantitative research approach was the major approach in our study because it was free from bias and helped us to explore the relationship of variables where the relationship between students' performance and learning and teaching process was investigated. The case study design was selected in order to have detailed information and a comprehensive picture on the factors contributing to students' academic performance in the selected schools by examining the trends of students' performance. Moreover, this type of research design was employed in this study because only one area was chosen for the study as was not possible to conduct a study that could cover the whole country. In this study, both quantitative and qualitative research approaches were employed for the purpose of obtaining detailed and variety of required information.

Samples and Sampling

In doing research, it is not possible for researchers to conduct research to everything relating to the problem. The researcher has to select few among the interesting study samples in order to study on behalf of the rest. This process of selecting the best samples for study is called *sampling*. Payne and Payne define sampling thus: "Sampling is the process of selecting a sub-set, of people or social phenomena to be studied, from the larger 'universe' to which they belong.. . . "[7] Following this understanding, our study targeted Headmasters, teachers and students in the three selected Community Secondary Schools whereby ten teachers were selected to participate in answering the questions, three Head Masters and fifteen students from each of the three selected schools—Itezi, Pankumbi

---

6. Singh, *Fundamentals of Research*, 150; Payne & Payne, *Key Concepts in Social Research*, 31–35.

7. Payne & Payne, *Key Concepts in Social Research*, 2019.

and Uyole Secondary Schools. This sample size was adequate to provide us the required information about our study.

What is sample size? Kothari defines sample size as the number of items to be selected from the universe to constitute a sample.[8] In this study, headmasters, teachers, and students from the three Community Secondary Schools at Uyole Village in Mbeya region were selected to represent the populations of those groups. A simple random sampling procedure was employed to select teachers and students who participated in the research study whereby from the identified Schools 15 students and 10 teachers in each of the three selected Schools were selected. The random sampling was used in this study because it provides all people equal chances and is the sampling which avoids bias; and 3 headmasters in the three schools were selected purposely since we considered that all of them had the required information.

Instrumentation and Data Processing

To investigate the results of this study two methods or instruments of data collection were used: questionnaires and interviews. The *Oxford Advanced Learners' Dictionary* of 2010 defines questionnaire as a written or printed list of questions to be answered by a number of people especially as part of survey OR It refers to the sets of questions given to respondents or informants in order for them to fill it. In this study a set of structured questions was provided to students and teachers. According to Orodho, questionnaires are appropriate in enabling the researcher gather a large amount of data from many subjects economically.[9] In our study, questionnaires were administered to specific groups of people—students and teachers—where papers were collected as soon as they finished filling them. This technique is important because it makes easy to acquire information from many people for a short

8. Kothari, *Research Methodology*
9. Orodho, *Techniques of Writing*

METHODOLOGICAL PERSPECTIVES

period of time; and there is greater anonymity and privacy of informants' information as well as freedom from bias.[10]

Moreover, Kothari defines an interview as the social encounter where speakers collaborate in producing retrospective and prospective accounts or version of their parts or future actions, experiences, feelings and thoughts.[11] In this study, the type of interview was interpersonal interview which involves an eye to eye interview between the interviewee and the interviewer.[12] The questions asked were in structured form which is easy to analyze. Hence, in this study, interview was done to students and teachers and the questions asked were structured.

On the one hand, the quantitative data collected in this study were analyzed using the Statistical Package for Social Sciences (SPSS) version 20 in coding, entry and analysis of data, and particularly the computation of frequencies, mean, cross tabulation and percentages. On the other hand, the qualitative data were analyzed descriptively by providing descriptions. The presentation of data obtained from the study was done in the form of words to obtain themes or central ideas contained in the segments of the grouped data. This way of handling qualitative data was executed because qualitative data involved the drawing of themes from experiences and meanings which informants made from those experiences. Therefore, the analysis of data was done in both quantitative and qualitative means, which helped us to obtain a variety of evidence about our study. Eventually, quantitatively analyzed data were presented in the form of tables and qualitative data were presented in the form of themes as will be clearly noted in the following chapter.

Ethical Considerations

Every human interaction has its ethical underpinnings which make it harmless and effective. This is the reality to any empirical

10. Cf. Mligo, *Introduction to Research*, 90.

11. Kothari, *Research Methodology*

12. Kothari, *Research Methodology, cf.* Mligo, *Introduction to Research*, 85; cf. Seidman, *Interviewing as a Qualitative Research*.

research. Iphofen writes thus about research ethics: "Behaving ethically when conducting research requires the researcher to plan a route through a moral maze. To engage in ethical research one constantly has to make choices within a range of options. These options involve competing principles, often in tension with each other, and which present us with moral dilemmas that are common to all research—not just social science."[13] This means that our research, as empirical research, also involved some options and choices within some ethical principles to safeguard the integrity of participants and research as a whole.

Before conducting the study we, as researchers, requested voluntary permission from the headmasters of the respective schools we were to collect data. We requested permission after receiving a letter from the District Education officer (DEO) to allow us to conduct research to those schools. The respondents were well-informed on the purpose of our study before commencing the data collection process. This is what entails of *informed consent* as Israel and Hay say "that research participants need to understand, first, that they are authorizing someone else to involve them in research and, second, what they are authorizing. Most commentators have concentrated on the second issue.... [R]esearchers need to provide potential participants with information about the purpose, methods, demands, risks, inconveniences, discomforts and possible outcomes of the research, including whether and how results might be disseminated."[14] This is mostly what was done before commencing our study process.

Moreover, as researchers, we strived to stay to the informants' own careful thoughts ensuring that the moral standards did not fail to respect their rights, dignity and well-being. In respecting the dignity of respondents, we followed the ethical principles, such as ensuring respondents' confidentiality by not including their names, institutions and photographs in the research report.[15]

---

13. Iphafen, *Ethical Decision-Making*, 7.
14. Israel & Hay, *Research Ethics*, 61; cf. Oliver, *The Students' Guide*, 28–30
15. Cf. Israel & Hay, *Research Ethics*, 78–80.

METHODOLOGICAL PERSPECTIVES

In following anonymity as an ethical principle, respondents' were handled by hiding their identity in the research report. Their names and places where they came from were represented by letters or numbers to make easier to explore issues which could be slightly unpopular, or which were regarded as sensitive.[16] Moreover, plagiarism was also handled carefully during our study. Plagiarism involves the use of another person's ideas or words without acknowledging the source of that material.[17] In handling the question of plagiarism, we ensured that all ideas and words from other people were duly acknowledged. Moreover, there was freedom of informants to continue participating or withdrawing from the study at any time if they felt to do so.[18] In this case, our research strived hard to avoid research misconduct in most of its occurrences.[19]

Conclusion

The major aim of this chapter was to lay down the procedures followed to obtain data from informants in order to deal with the problem of academic performance in Community Secondary Schools in Tanzania. Four important aspects have been discussed in this chapter: the scope of research and the design used, the samples and sampling procedures adopted, the instruments for

16. Israel & Hay, *Research Ethics*, 5.

17. Oliver, *Students' Guide*, 132-136; Mligo, *Writing Academic Papers*, 63-87.

18. Cf. Israel & Hay, *Research Ethics*, 30-31.

19. Research misconduct appears in various forms, e.g., fabrication, falsification, and plagiarism. The "Federal Policy on Research Misconduct" of the United States Office of Science and Technology Policy defines each of these terms as follows: "'Fabrication' is making up data or results and recording or reporting them. 'Falsification' is manipulating research materials, equipment or processes, or changing or omitting data or results such that the research is not accurately represented in the research record. 'Plagiarism' is the appropriation of another person's ideas, processes, results or words without giving appropriate credit.. . . " (Iphofen, *Ethical Decision-Making*, 211, cf. Israel & Hay, *Research Ethics*, 113).

data collection of research data and how the processing of data was done after their collection, and the ethical issues considered during the research process. In laying out the procedures for the research process, we believe that readers of this book will be able to ascertain the way the data discussed in the following chapter were obtained and processed.

Chapter 4

CURRENT STATE OF ACADEMIC PERFORMANCE

Findings and Discussions

Introduction

IN ORDER TO MAKE THE RESEARCH COMPLETE, findings should be communicated in order to argue one's case. In order to argue our case, this chapter comprises of findings on the factors contributing to students' poor performance in Community Secondary Schools whereby a study was done at three Community Secondary Schools in Uyole-Village. The chapter is divided into four parts: the background characteristics of respondents, factors contributing to students' poor performance, causes of students' absenteeism, challenges and factors contributing to students' poor performance from both teachers and students and the trends of national form four examination results in the selected schools. The data obtained have been presented both quantitatively in terms of tables, frequencies and percentages and qualitatively in terms of themes and descriptions. The data were collected by using questionnaires as a tool of data collection, where by questionnaires were administered to 78 respondents and about 96.2% returned the questionnaires out of 100%. Therefore, the data analysis, presentation and discussion is done in relation to the two theoretical perspectives discussed in chapter two (organization and motivation theories) and the returned questionnaires and interviews conducted from the research area.

Respondents and Responses

In this section we first present the respondents who participated in the study and the responses they provided in the research process, especially during the questionnaire administration.

Questionnaires Return Rate

Questionnaires were administered to three secondary schools: Pankumbi, Itezi and Uyole secondary schools. In each of the three selected schools, 15 students, 10 teachers and one head of school were selected. However, responses were as shown in table 1 below.

Table 1: Questionnaires Return Rate

Respondents	X Secondary School	Y Secondary School	Z Secondary School
Heads of School	1	1	1
Teachers	10	7	10
Students	15	15	15

Source: Field Data, May–June 2017

Table 1 above shows that there was low response of questionnaires from teachers in one of the selected schools. This low response caused a shortage of some of the information needed for this study. Despite this shortage, the obtained responses were sufficient to generalize the obtained results to the teachers' population.

CURRENT STATE OF ACADEMIC PERFORMANCE

Genders and Ages of Respondents

The concept of gender has been defined in various ways depending on contexts. This concept has in most cases been confused with the concept of sex. Unity and Igbudu have defined gender as follows: "Gender is the range of physical, biological, mental and behavioural characteristics pertaining to and differentiating between masculinity and feminity.... Depending on the context, the term may refer to biological sex (i.e. the state of being male, female or intersex), sex based social structure (including gender roles and other social roles) or gender identity . . . ."[1] This research included both males and females for the aim of avoiding to hide the information according to gender. To students, females were about 46.7% and males were about 53.3%; to teachers, males where about 55.6% and females were about 44.4%; and to heads of schools, females where about 33.3% and males where about 66.7%. This distribution indicates that the gender issue was taken seriously in this study. However, this gender consideration did not mean to indicate that one gender orientation had better performance than the other.

About the ages of respondents, the ages of students ranging from 13–17 were about 55.6% and the ages ranging from 17–20 were about 44.4%; to teachers, the ages ranging from 20–30 were about 22.2%, the ages ranging from 31–40 were about 55.6% and the age ranging from 41–50 were about 22.2%, the ages of the heads of schools were of the same range ranging from 30–40 which was about 100%. The gender and ages of respondents involved in this study are presented in table 2 below. Viewed more closely, the ages and genders of respondents were at their most active stage.

---

1. Unity & Igbudu, "Influence of Gender," 101.

Table 2: Genders and Ages of Respondents

		Frequency	Percent
Students	Female	21	46.7
	Male	24	53.3
	Total	45	100.0
Teachers	Male	15	50.0
	Female	12	40.0
	Total	27	90.0
	Missing system	3	10.0
	Total	30	100.0
Heads of Schools	Male	2	66.7
	Female	1	33.3
	Total	3	100.0
Ages of Respondents	13–16 years	25	55.6
	17–20 years	20	44.4
	Total	45	100.0
Students Teachers' ages	20–30 years	6	20.0
	31–40 years	15	50.0
	41–50 years	6	20.0
	Total	27	90.0
	Missing system	3	10.0
	Total	30	100.0
Heads of School	30–40 years	3	100.0

Source: Field Data, May–June 2017

CURRENT STATE OF ACADEMIC PERFORMANCE

There are opposing views among scholars about the contribution of age of students to academic performance. Some scholars view that there is a relationship between age of students and academic performance[2] while others see that there is no any relationship between the two factors.[3] We should clearly state here that our indication of ages of respondents in this study does not aim at determining the relationship in performance in terms of ages of respondents. Our aim is to show that most respondents in this study were of active age ranges. To our study, this indication means that age was not the factor used to measure students' or teachers' academic performance.

Academic Qualifications of Students, Teachers, and Heads of Schools

Tope asserts that "Teacher's competency enhances a teacher's ability to create an environment that is fair, understanding, and accepting of diverse students, ideas, experiences, and backgrounds. Teachers have been found to be the single most important factor influencing student achievement."[4] In this study, academic qualification was one of the questions asked in the questionnaires administered to students, teachers, and heads of schools. The responses of these groups of respondents about their academic qualifications are shown in tables 3 and 4 below:

2. Momanyi, Too & Simiyu, "Effect of Students' Age"; Jabor et al., "The Influence of Age."
3. Voyles, "Student Academic Success"; Ebenuwa-Okoh, "Influence of Age."
4. Tope, *Effects of Teachers' Competence*, 5.

Table 3: Forms which Students Belonged

Students	Frequency	Percent
Form One	3	6.7
Form Two	1	2.2
Form Three	26	57.8
Form Five	15	33.3
Total	45	100.0

Table 4: Academic Qualifications of Teachers and Heads of Schools

Academic Qualification	Teachers' Frequency	Teachers' Percent	Heads of Schools' Frequency	Heads of Schools' Percents
Primary Education	-	-	-	-
Secondary Education	4	13.3	-	-
University Education	22	73.3	3	100.0
Total	26	86.7		100.0
Missing systems	4	13.3		
Total	30	100.0		
Others (diploma)				

Source: Field data, May–June 2017

Table 4 above shows that a large number of teachers had university education qualification which was about 73.3% of the teachers holding university degree, and about 13.3% teachers having secondary education. Although a large number of teachers held university degrees, the above findings show that still they did not have enough skills and knowledge to cope with the changes in the education curriculum. The above findings show that having university qualifications alone hardly guarantees teachers' competency/quality in the teaching profession. Teacher quality is an accumulation of skills to enhance performance. Teachers' quality/competency becomes manifest in the performance of those being taught. The findings suggest that there is a need for teachers to advance their skills and knowledge in order to cope with the changes in the system of education after graduating from colleges and universities in order to build more competency and meet the evolving trends in education.

Similar results were obtained in a research conducted by Kafyulilo. Kafyulilo notes that there has been an alarming decline in performance of science subjects in the country for both primary and secondary schools, especially Mathematics, which leads to few students who select to participate in science subjects. In his words, Kafyulilo further adds: "While the country is in a great demand for engineers, doctors, accountants, science and mathematics teachers as well as agricultural officers, the percentage of students engaging in science and mathematics subjects in secondary schools is decreasing year after year.... Poor performance and participation in Science and Mathematics has been attributed to among others, the teachers' inadequate competencies in science and mathematics, a lack of science teaching and learning resources and a shortage of science and mathematics teachers in most schools. ... Teachers are especially found to have limited competencies in science and mathematics teaching skills (the pedagogical knowledge) and the knowledge of the technological tools that can support learning ...."[5] Therefore, in regard to the above statement, the poor quality of education qualifications to teachers contribute to students' poor performance. Laddunuri in his research also holds the same view that poor education hardly helps one to cope up with changes in the curriculum and serve properly.[6]

Another cause of students' failure is when teachers teach subjects which they have no experiences with or failed during their studies. A good example is when a teacher studied teaching History but he or she goes to teach Mathematics instead; it is obvious that the products of that teacher will be poor. Similarly, Muhonyiwa asserts that one wonders how a teacher who failed in his/her

---

5. Kafyulilo, "Professional Development," 672, cf. Tope, *The Effect of Teachers' Competence*.
6. Laddunuri, "Status of School."

academic subject can teach others the subject he or she failed in examinations without producing failures.[7] This calls for teachers to change their practice; they should teach according to competences and specializations in order to enhance better delivery of materials to students.

Another aspect which leads to poor performance of students is teachers' lack of self-satisfaction; it is their unwillingness to collaborate in uplifting their teaching skills and competences. Kafyulilo asserts that one of the most effective aspects in leading to the development of teachers' competences is the collaboration among themselves in raising these competences. However, Kafyulilo notes that collaboration is the most lacking of all aspects among teachers, which eventually leads to lack of innovation to these teachers.[8] Lack of effective collaboration in order to share what they have among themselves affects students' academic outcomes.

Years of Schools' Establishment

In this study, we also sought data on the year of school establishment to help us identify schools which had stayed for a long time and still had poor academic performances. It was our assumption that being established a long time could help such schools to discover the factors for their poor performance and lead them to rectifying such factors. For such schools established for a long time and were still having poor performance, our question wanted to determine the factors which led such schools stay such a long time without rectifying their poor performance in examinations.

Table 5 below shows that all selected schools in the research area were established more than ten years past, which was sufficient enough for them to observe the factors contributing to students' poor performance and taking measures to improve their performance. Therefore, this result shows that there was a negative

---

7. Muhonyiwa, "Factors influencing Poor Examination Performance."
8. Kafyulilo, Professional Development, 674.

relationship between the years for the schools' establishments and the students' academic performance.

Table 5: Years of Schools' Establishment

Secondary school	Year of school establishment
X Secondary School	2002
Y Secondary School	2007
Z secondary School	2004

Source: Field Data, May–June 2017

Students' Performance according to Gender

In our research we also determined whether the gender of students had any relationship with the poor academic performance of students in Community Secondary Schools. The results are presented in the table below.

Table 6: Academic Performance according to Gender

	Frequency	Percentage
Girls	4	13.3
Boys	15	50.0
None	8	26.7
Total	27	90.0
Missing systems	3	10.3
Total	30	100

Source: Field Data, May–June 2017

The table of performance above (table 6) shows that about 13.3% of respondents said that girls performed well in their studies; moreover, about 50.0% of respondents indicate that boys were those who performed well in their studies, and about 26.7% of the respondents indicate that none of them who performed well in their studies, which means that neither girls nor boys performed well in their studies. These results show that in the selected schools boys were the ones who performed well in their studies. However, other studies have indicated that gender orientations have fewer effects on performance despite the fact that boys and girls have different behaviors in classroom.[9]

Years of Experience of Teachers and Heads of Schools

Experience of the heads of schools and other teachers contributed to students' poor performance depending on the years that they stayed in their stations. We asked respondents about the relationship between the experience of individual teachers and the academic performance of their students. The table below indicates the years of experience to both teachers and heads of schools in the selected schools.

Table 7: Teachers' Years of Experience

Years of experience	Frequency	Percent
0–5 years	10	33.3
6–10 years	5	16.7
11–15 years	7	23.3
16–20 years	3	10.0
Over 20 years	1	3.3
Total	26	86.7
Missing system	4	13.3
Total	30	100.0

Source: Field Data, May–June 2017

Most teachers from the schools surveyed had 0–5 years of working experience which is about 33.3%, followed by teachers who had 11–15 years which is about 23.3%. This experience is believed to be enough for handling administrative issues as well as

---

9. Cf. Voyles, "Student Academic Success," 73; Joseph, et al., "Effect of Gender."

the learning process of students by improving their performance. These findings correspond with Adeyemi's research in Ondo State, Nigeria to determine the relationship between teachers' teaching experience and students' performance outcomes. He found out that "Schools having more teachers with five years and above teaching experience achieved better results than schools having more teachers with less than five years teaching experience."[10]

Moreover, the heads of schools, whose years of experience was above ten years, had enough experience for improving school administration so as to ensure better performance of their students in examinations taking into account that the school administration was a crucial factor in the success of a school performance. The heads of schools were in a position to ensure that all factors within the schools that make the schools environment favorable for the learning process including ensuring sufficient school facilities are maintained so as to ensure quality educational standards.

The results above show that heads of schools and teachers staying for a long time in their station was not a factor which made them take measures to address the problem of poor performance in their schools. Despite their long stay at their respective schools, still there was a problem of poor performance in those schools. Following the above findings, we argue that there is a need for teachers and the heads of schools to study well about their schools, especially those factors contributing to students' poor performance in their respective schools at the time they are in those schools. Factors like school administrations, teachers' and students' motivations, school environment and supply of learning and teaching materials are crucial factors contributing to students' performance which need their effective scrutiny despite the long experiences of teachers and heads of schools.

---

10. Adeyemi, "Teachers' Teaching Experience," 204, cf. Mligo & Mwashilind, *English as a Language of Teaching and Learning*, 91–92; Yusuf & Dada, "Impact of Teachers' Qualification" ; Ewetan & Ewetan, "Teachers' Teaching Experience"; Dial, "The effect of Teacher Experience"; Akiri, "Effects of Teachers' Effectiveness"; Clement, "Factors influencing the Academic Performance"; Magati, Bosire & Ogeta, "Factors affecting Academic Performance."

Size of Classrooms and Academic Performance

The number of students in classrooms is an important factor to look at when addressing the issue of learning process because the size of classroom has an effect on the process of teaching and learning. Teachers were asked on the number of students in their classrooms and how that class size affected students' performance. Their responses are documented in table 8 below.

Table 8: Sizes of Classrooms and Students' Academic Performance

		Frequency	Percent
Valid	Very big (above 50)	7	23.3
	Big (between 40-50)	15	50.0
	Moderate (between 30-40)	4	13.3
	Small (below 30)	1	3.3
	Total	27	90.0
Missing System		3	10.0
Total		30	100.0

Source: Field Data, May–June, 2017

The results above show that most of the teachers, about 50% of teachers, handled big classes which had between 40–50 students. This number made it difficult for teachers to handle such large numbers of students in one class, which made them unable to interact with their students effectively on individual basis. This inability to interact made them unable to realize when they were absent in classes. Moreover, about 23.3% of respondents indicated that they handled very big classes which had above 50 students, about 13.3% indicated that they handled moderate classes which had about 30–40 students and some few teachers about 3.3% indicated that they handled classes which were below 30 students.

CURRENT STATE OF ACADEMIC PERFORMANCE

In the activity which involves interaction between people to enhance learning to take place, the question of ratio between teachers and students is crucial. We therefore agree that handling big class sizes have negative relationships on students' performance because big classes cause difficulty for teachers to interact with students at individual basis in order to know their presence in classes and their comprehension of the taught content. Moreover, students face difficulties to write and some students hardly understand well things taught by their teachers. Okumbe also had a similar observation that overcrowding in classrooms makes it difficult for pupils to write and the teacher may also be unable to move around and help the needy pupils.[11] Therefore, handling small classes comfortably is a way of identifying weak learners through marking assignments and home works, which eventually enhances students' comprehension of the content taught.

However, from the above results about the size of classes, there were also some teachers who indicated that the size of classes in their schools affected students' academic performance and others disagreed that the size of classroom did not affect students' academic performance. This disagreement is as shown in the table below.

Table 9: Does the Number of Students in Class affect Their Academic Performance?

	Frequency	Percent
Yes	17	56.7
No	9	30.0
Total	26	86.7
Missing systems	4	13.3
Total	30	100.0

Source: Field Data, May–June 2017

---

11. Okumbe, *Educational Management*, cf. Vandenberg, "Class Size and Academic Achievement."

The findings of this study in table 9 above show that the size of students in classes was one of the factors which contributed to students' poor performance in the investigated Community Secondary Schools. About 56% of the teachers said 'yes' that the size of the classroom may sometimes affect students' performance, while about 30% of teachers said 'No' which means that the size of the class is not the factor which affects students' performance. The above division of respondents indicates the contextual nature of the teaching process. Teaching which takes place in one place is not necessarily the same as the one taking place in another place. There is also disagreement among scholars on the effectiveness of class sizes as a factor for effective performance among students. There are those who see the relationship between class size and students' performance[12] and those who do not see this relationship.[13]

However, as researchers, we are of the opinion that the large number of students in the classroom is one of the factors contributing to students' poor performance because it makes teachers unable to move around to help the needs of pupils, teachers face difficulty to identify absenteeism to students, students' loss of attention during learning due to noises and murmuring, shortage of learning resources as well as difficulty in evaluating students' performance. With a similar view, Bascia also found that large classes made it difficult for teachers to monitor pupils' attendance, encouraging pupils' absenteeism and making the learning process ineffective.[14] Therefore, there is a need to set the adequate number of students in classrooms which make easy for teachers to handle and monitor for effective learning and teaching process. This adequate class makes easy for students to learn comfortably and contributes to students' better performance in their schools.

12. E.g., Vandenberg, "Class Size and Academic Performance."
13. E.g., Uhrain, "Effect of Class Size."
14. Bascia, *Achieving Universal Primary Education*.

CURRENT STATE OF ACADEMIC PERFORMANCE

General Academic Performance

As we have indicated in the findings above, performance of students always depends on the various factors. The table below shows the general performance of the surveyed schools in their summative examinations as was responded by teachers.

Table 10: General Academic Performance in Form Four National Examinations

		Frequency	Percent
Valid	Very good	1	3.3
	Good	4	13.3
	Moderate	13	43.3
	Poor	9	30.0
	Total	27	90.0
Missing System		3	10.0
Total		30	100.0

Source:FieldData

About 3.3% of the teachers indicated that the general academic performance in their schools was very good, about 13.3% of teachers indicated that their academic performance of national examination was good, about 43.3% of the teachers indicated that the general performance of national examination was moderate and about 30% of the teachers indicated that the general performance of national examination was poor. The above results show that respondents who see performance to be moderate and poor are more than those who consider it to be very good and good.

Laddunuri's research also found that the mushrooming of secondary schools in Tanzania, especially Community Secondary Schools, led to lack of qualified teachers to teach in those schools, which eventually led to massive failures of students.[15] The above responses and Laddunuri's findings indicate that more efforts are needed by the government and respective school administrations

15. Laddunuri, "Status of School."

to examine the factors contributing towards moderate performance and not good performance. There is a need for improving school environments to both teachers and students, ensuring the provision of enough facilities and all learning materials to support their learning and teaching processes; these are the main factors which most likely contribute to the increase or decrease of students' performance.

Rewards to Students and Their Study Habit

From the findings obtained in this study, it was shown that more students, about 60%, indicated that they were given rewards such as books, pens, pencils which encouraged them to study hard and help those who were not studying hard to concentrate in studying so that they could acquire such rewards, while about 40% disagreed that they did not provide rewards to those who performed well in their studies. Therefore, this shows that to some extent rewards is one of the factors which contribute to students' better performance. The results obtained are shown in the table below.

Table 11: Do you Provide Rewards to Students who perform Better?

	Frequency	Percent
Yes	27	60.0
No	18	40.0
Total	45	100.0

Source: Field Data, May–June 2017

Studies from other researchers also support the above findings that, in some cases, providing some rewards to students due to performance can promote students better performance.[16] However, other studies discourage the provision of rewards to students because it divides them between the few capable who will be highly motivated and the majority incapable who will be lowly motivated.

16. Cf. Pierce, et al., "Positive Effects of Rewards."

CURRENT STATE OF ACADEMIC PERFORMANCE

Those who are highly motivated will continue to perform better and those who are lowly motivated will continue to be discouraged.[17] Baranek for example, writes thus about the effectiveness of rewards to students: "Students with learning disabilities are very often unmotivated because school is one failure after another to them.. . . When rewards are given, they often have the opposite effect of what was intended. High student achievement comes from students who are motivated from inside. Therefore, instead of giving rewards, teachers need to consistently teach students to become intrinsically motivated."[18] The negative effects of rewards to students reported by researches above indicate the need for teachers to enhance students have intrinsic motivation instead of relying on the physical rewards that demoralize more than provide academic moral support.

Presence of Subject Clubs and Academic Performance

Table 12 below shows that most students indicated that in their schools there were subject clubs which was about of 95.6% of the students; whereby, clubs was one of the factors which build students minds by exchanging ideas with their fellow students as well as building confidence which could lead them to perform well in their studies; however, about 4.4% disagreed that in their schools there was no subject clubs.

Table 12: Presence of Subject Clubs in Community Secondary Schools

	Frequency	Percent
Yes	43	95.6
No	2	4.4
Total	45	100.0

Source: Field Data, May–June 2017

17. Leuven, Oosterbeek & Klaauw, "The effects of Financial Rewards"; Baranek, "The effects of Rewards."
18. Baranek, "The effects of Rewards," 3.

Moreover, the table below shows the clubs which students were, whereby most students indicated that they were in natural science clubs which was about 35.6% of students, about 17.8% of students indicated that they were in social science subjects, and about 20.0% indicated that they were in applied science subjects. However, other students mentioned other clubs which were engaging with arts clubs such as history, English, Kiswahili, civics, and environment clubs. Having subject clubs is one of the factors which may contribute in some extents to students' better performance because clubs build students' confidence, interact with other students by exchanging their ideas which is helpful in their studies and expanding students' minds to think about different issues related to their studies.

Table 13: Clubs which Students were Enrolled

Subjects	Frequency	Percent
Natural Science	16	35.6
Social Science	8	17.8
Applied Science	9	20.0
Total	23	73.3
Missing system	12	26.7
Total	45	100.0

Source: Field Data, May–June 2017

National Examination Results for Surveyed Community Secondary Schools

After discussing the respondents and their responses on various issues causing poor academic performance among students in Community Secondary Schools in the above paragraphs, this section presents and discusses the performance trends of students in the surveyed schools for five years (2011—2016). This presentation helps in discussing the various challenges which influence students' academic performance in the surveyed schools.

CURRENT STATE OF ACADEMIC PERFORMANCE

Form Four Results Trend for X Secondary School (2011—2016)

Table 14 below shows the national examination results of form four at X Secondary School performance trend. The results show that in each year there was a great number of students who scored division four and division zero as compared to those students who scored division one, two and three. Generally, the performance was not good because of the decreasing trend of students who passed with division one to three in respective years; and who normally qualifies for enrollment in advanced level education. This implies that, the school contributes fewer students to the number of students enrolled in advanced level.

Table 14: X Secondary School Form Four Examination Results Trend (2011—2016)

	Division 1		Division II		Division III		Division IV		Division O		Total
Year	Boys	Girls	Boys	Girls	Boys	Girls	Boys	Girls	Boys	Girls	
2011	4	0	5	0	11	3	42	35	27	21	176
2012	0	0	3	0	11	3	52	44	83	78	274
2013	2	1	17	9	13	20	33	38	36	40	209
2014	1	0	18	9	20	12	46	58	21	18	203
2015	4	0	13	11	25	21	57	84	39	54	308
2016	2	0	4	9	21	18	44	61	32	61	252

Source: Field Data, May–June 2017

From the results of X secondary school above, there is a need to the school administration to put more efforts on those factors contributing to students' poor performance. Most of the factors contributing to students' poor performance as observed from this school include poor learning environment, shortage of facilities, problem of absenteeism, shortage of teachers, poor cooperation between students, parents and teachers which should be addressed so as to have better performance. Moreover, the government should take its part in ensuring the presence of enough teachers especially science teachers; and there should be enough facilities in Community Secondary Schools.

Form Four Results Trend for Y Secondary School (2011—2016)

As shown in table 22 below, the form four examination results for the Y Secondary School did not well improve year by year. In 2011, 2012, 2013, 2014, 2015 and 2016 the divisions four and zero were high as compared to divisions one, two and three which were the results that could at least allow a student to proceed for advanced secondary school education. These results show that all the years 2011 to 2016, fewer students from X Secondary School pass to form five advanced secondary education.

Table 15: Y Secondary School Form Four Examination Results Trend (2011-2016)

Year	Division 1		Division II		Division III		Division IV		Division O		Total
	Boys	Girls	Boys	Girls	Boys	Girls	Boys	Girls	Boys	Girls	
2011	1	0	3	0	1	5	30	23	35	31	129
2012	1	0	1	0	5	1	27	16	48	40	139
2013	3	0	8	1	10	5	28	25	34	32	146
2014	1	0	4	0	5	6	24	29	11	12	92
2015	1	0	6	1	6	6	38	32	57	62	209
2016	0	0	5	1	6	7	36	45	60	54	214

Source: Field Data, May–June 2017

CURRENT STATE OF ACADEMIC PERFORMANCE

From the results of Y secondary school above, as it was to the school X, there is a need to the school administration to look on the factors contributing to students poor performance in their schools, where most of the factors contributing to students poor performance as observed from this schools are poor learning environment, shortage of facilities, problem of absenteeism, shortage of teachers, poor cooperation between students, parents and teachers all these should be addressed so as to have better performance. In addition, there is a need for the government to address the problem available in Community Secondary Schools such as ensuring the presence of enough facilities and teachers to facilitate better performance.

Form Four Results Trend for Z Secondary School (2011-2016)

Form four examination results for Z Secondary School show that their performance was not good. In 2011 there was no any division one, only two division two and four division three which was only 5% of the students were having the chance to be enrolled to proceed with Advanced Level studies whereby 95% failed. Even in 2012, 2013, 2014, 2015 and 2016 more than seventy percent of candidates were found to have division four and zero. The results also indicate that a very limited number of students qualified to pursue advanced level secondary education. Table 23 below indicates the performance trend of Z Secondary School.

Table 16: Z Secondary School Form Four Examination Results Trend (2011—2016)

Year	Division 1		Division II		Division III		Division IV		Division O		Total
	Boys	Girls	Boys	Girls	Boys	Girls	Boys	Girls	Boys	Girls	
2011	0	0	2	0	4	0	36	23	30	27	122
2012	1	0	6	1	8	1	34	21	41	35	148

COMMUNITY SECONDARY SCHOOLS IN TANZANIA

Year	Division 1		Division II		Division III		Division IV		Division O		Total
2013	2	0	6	1	9	7	27	24	24	17	117
2014	2	0	11	1	11	4	30	34	21	9	93
2015	1	1	8	4	18	2	31	37	34	30	209
2016	0	0	6	0	21	16	42	31	37	32	185

Source: Field Data, May–June 2017

The examination results in X, Y and Z secondary schools above correspond to the findings of David in his research at Sumbawanga District.[19] In two of the schools he surveyed, the following were the results: "The students' scores of Msanzi secondary schools shows [sic!] that; out of 669 candidates who sat for CSEE for five year only division one was only one candidate 0.15%, division two 3 candidates 0.45%, division three (21) 3.14%, division four (214) 31.99% and division zero was (430) 64.27%. Matai secondary school students score reveals that from 562 candidates; division one was zero, division two it was (7) 1.25%, division three (33) 5.87%), division four (272) 48.34% and division zero was (250) 44.48%."[20]

The results in our study area and those of David's research above show exactly that most Community Secondary Schools in Tanzania have inadequate academic performance considering the factors contributing to students poor performance as mentioned by students of these schools, which include truancy, shortage of facilities, and shortage of teachers. From the results of Z secondary school, as is to the two other schools above, there is a need for the school administration to address the factors contributing to students' poor performance in their schools so as to have better academic performance. Most factors contributing to students' poor performance as observed from these schools include poor learning environment, shortage of facilities, problem of absenteeism,

---

19. See David, "Determinants of Poor Academic Performance," 66–68.
20. David, "Determinants of Poor Academic Performance," 66.

shortage of teachers, and poor cooperation between students, parents and teachers.

Environmental Challenges influencing Students' Academic Performance

After discussing the performance trends of the surveyed schools in the previous section, this section discusses two challenges which mostly face Community Secondary Schools leading them to students' failures in their summative examinations: lack of adequate teaching and learning facilities, and lack of adequate learning and teaching environments.

Lack of adequate Teaching and Learning Facilities

It was important for the study to analyze the learning and teaching facilities in terms of quality and quantity. The results obtained from this study show that most students complained that in their schools there were inadequate teaching and learning facilities such as lack of textbooks, reference books, teaching guides, supplementary books, journals, magazines and newspapers which were factors contributing to their poor performance. Moreover, about 35.6% of students agreed that in their schools there was enough facilities to facilitate the learning process while about 64.4% disagreed that in their school there were no enough facilities to facilitate the learning process. This shows that there is a great relationship between teaching and learning facilities to students' academic performance. According to this data, there was poor performance in most of the Community Secondary Schools because of the shortage of enough facilities to facilitate their learning. Students mostly depended on what their teachers taught them and what they wrote in the teaching notes.

Table 17: Are Facilities to facilitate Learning and Teaching Process available?

	Frequency	Percent
Yes	16	35.6
No	29	64.4
Total	45	100.0

Source: Field Data, May–June 2017

Similar results are reported by David in his research in Sumbawanga District, Rukwa Region. David found that the Book/Students ratio was very low causing students to have difficulties in their studies, hence causing poor performance in examinations. David reports: "District Secondary Education Officer (DSEO) of Sumbawanga District Council reported that students: book Ratio in Sumbawanga District secondary schools was 11: 1 in 2012. Students books ratio in various subjects were as follows; Mathematics 1:4, Civics 1: 20, Chemistry 1:6, Physics 1: 5, Biology 1:2 and History 1:15, Geography 1:14, English 1:11 and Kiswahili 1: 11 respectively. Therefore, the average Students-book Ratio (SBR) in Sumbawanga District was 1: 11 at the end of the year 2012 (DSEO, 2012)."[21]

The above findings by David indicate that a library with enough and relevant teaching and learning materials is important for students' better performance. If the library is lacking, it should not be expected that excellent performance will be achieved because students and teachers will not have appropriate sources of their knowledge. David further states thus about the library:

> a library [is] a building or room in which collection of books, tapes, newspapers, journals; and articles are kept for people to read study or borrow. Library is an essential factor in the teaching-learning process. It forms one of the most important educational services. The

---

21. David, "Determinants of Poor Academic Performance, 55; cf. Clement, ""Factors influencing the Academic Performance"; Magati, Bosire & Ogeta, "Factors affecting Academic Performance."

CURRENT STATE OF ACADEMIC PERFORMANCE

educational process functions in a world of books. The chief purpose of a school library is to make available to the pupil, at his easy convenience, all books, periodicals and other reproduced materials which are of interest and value to him but which are not provided or assigned to him as basic or supplementary textbooks."[22]

Therefore, there is a need for the government to ensure that in all Community Secondary Schools there are enough facilities to facilities the teaching and learning process, for example adequate and appropriate laboratories with enough equipment for students to learn science, libraries with enough books to learn the existing knowledge and create the new one, and all materials related to learning and teaching process. Kipkoech observed that the availability and quality of textbooks in a secondary school library is an essential factor in the teaching-learning process because it will strongly lead to a better attainment of good performance. In other words, operating a learning institution without a well-equipped library is similar to having a big head without brain because the library is the brain of the institution.[23]

Poor Learning and Teaching Environment

This study also analyzed the learning and teaching environment as one of the factors that may affect students' academic performance in any secondary schools. Most students in the selected schools agreed that the environment was not conducive for them in their learning process because of the shortage of laboratories, libraries, etc. This shortage was one of the factors which caused the decrease in the school performance. Other students said that their environments were not conducive for them to learn, while others stated that their environments were conducive for them to learn. About 51.1% of students indicated that their environments were not conducive for them to learn; this was a large number as compared to those who indicated that their environments were conducive for

22. David, "Determinants of Poor Academic Performance," 30.
23. Kipkoech, "Influence of Socio-Economic Background."

them to learn—which was about 48.9 %. This is illustrated in the table below.

Table 18: Conduciveness of the Environment for Learning

	Frequency	Percent
Yes	22	48.9
No	23	51.1
Total	45	100.0

Source: Field Data, May–June 2017

Moreover, teachers indicated the conduciveness of environments during their teaching process. Here about 40.7% of teachers indicated that environments were conducive for their teaching process while about 51.9% indicated that environments were not conducive for their teaching process, and about 7.4% did not indicate whether the environment is conducive or not conducive for them to enhance better teaching. The data above mean that adequate teaching was not done due to poor teaching environment. Consequently, students could not attain the required content leading them into failure in summative examinations.

Moreover, David in his research at Sumbawanga Region in Tanzania noted: "The system of education in Tanzania presently faces disasters in terms of resources and management in particular. Teachers are demoralized, primary infrastructure is still facing many challenges (especially the quality of buildings, play grounds, the availability of teaching and learning material). The curriculum is lacking some relevance too."[24] This environmental inadequacy is the characteristic of most secondary schools within and outside the country which requires urgent attention.[25]

---

24. David, "Deaterminants of Poor Academic Performance," 14.

25. Cf. Jovinius, "An Investigation of the Effect of Geographical Location"; Chukwuemeka, "Environmental Influence"; Arshad & Ahmed, "Impact of Breakfast"; Clement, "Factors influencing the Academic Performance"; Magati, Bosire & Ogeta, "Factors affecting Academic Performance"; Nyamubi, "Determinants of Secondary School Teachers' Job Satisfaction."

Table 19: Teachers' Findings on the Conduciveness of the Environment

	Frequency	Percent
Yes	11	36.7
No	14	46.7
Total	25	83.3
Missing System	5	16.7
Total	30	100.0

Source: Field Data

At this point, we strongly agree that poor environment is one of the major factors contributing to students' poor performance. In order to improve the learning environment there is a need for the government, schools administration and other education stakeholders to create conducive environments which will encourage students to study hard and teachers do their work effectively. This encouragement will enhance better attainment of quality education for better performance in examinations and in the work fields after students' completion of studies. In regard to this point, Boma contends that improving quality and quantity of school learning environment will normally improve attendance, academic performance and completion rates.[26]

The Challenge of Absenteeism and Its Causes: Students' Opinions

Absenteeism is one of the major factors which cause failures in examinations. There are many factors which cause students' absenteeism; some are social, economical and others are cultural ones. According to Ayodele, "Absenteeism is common across university classes. Some of the reasons cited in the literature are illness, tiredness, prioritizing other academic work, anticipation of low academic gain, lack of interest/motivation or boredom. ... A major reason for student absenteeism in classes might be the

26. Boma, "Factors affecting Performance."

availability of online material, access to PowerPoint presentations, and YouTube."²⁷ However, most students from the selected schools mentioned some of the factors which caused students' absenteeism to be the following: punishments and harsh treatments, poverty, sickness, cooperation between students, teachers and parents, and students' ignorance.

Punishments and Harsh Treatments

Punishment is one of the tools which parents at homes and teachers at schools use in order to control the behavior of children. The main point towards the execution of punishment is to create fear to the one being punished in order to prevent him/her from repeating a certain undesirable behavior. In schools, there are a variety of punishments provided to students. Punishments are divided into two main groups: positive and negative punishments. Positive punishments inflict pain upon the student making that student not repeat a particular unwanted behavior, such punishments include canning the misbehaved student, providing them some physical activities (e.g., watering school garden and uprooting some tree logs around the school), farming in the school farms, kneeling on rough surfaces of the earth, doing push-ups, and seating in one place for a long time. The positive punishments at schools include restricting the student from attending classes for some time because of misbehavior. At their homes, children may be canned for not implementing directions, not attending schools, stealing, etc. (positive punishments) or restricted from watching television because of not doing poor performance at school. All these mentioned punishments or treatments aim at motivating the student not to repeat a particular behavior. Therefore, motivations in the form of punishments are treatments which students receive in order to create to them fear of repeating the behavior which is not required.²⁸

27. Ayodele, "Class Attendance," 64.
28. Cf. Suleman, Aslam & Singh, "Effects of Mild Corporal Punishment"; Ehiane, "Discipline and Academic Performance," 183–184; Invocavity, "The

In this study, most of the students reported that punishments and harsh treatments were factors which mostly caused students' absenteeism in school. About 68.8% of students reported that punishments and harsh treatments where the major causes of the problem of absenteeism which in turn caused poor performance in their results because they did not participate well in their studies. Therefore, there is a great relationship between students' punishments and harsh treatments of students and their absenteeism and which leads to poor academic performance in most Community Secondary School. We strongly agree that punishment and harsh treatment are not one of the factors which increase students' motivation towards their better performance more than educating them friendly to enhance an inward motivation. Punishment should be executed when it is needed to return a student to a straight line, but not too much. When parents and teachers use corporal punishment as an attempt to reduce an emerging unacceptable behaviors adopted by their children, the long term effect tend to be further increased as the children continue with those unacceptable behaviors. This means that the punishment done helps very little towards rectifying the students' unacceptable behaviors.

Poverty and Sickness

The results obtained from students show that students' absenteeism was mostly caused by poverty from their families. About 33.3% of teachers mentioned poverty of parents as being the cause of students' absenteeism. There are students who come from poor families who were unable to afford school needs, for example uniforms, bicycles for students to use as a means of transport, and even providing pocket money for students to buy meals not provided by schools, especially for day students. This made them not

---

effect of Corporal Punishment," 14–15; Yaghambe, "Disciplinary Networks"; Hassan & Bali, "Assessing the effects of Corporal Punishment."

attend schools regularly making it difficult for them to understand what were taught in their respective classes during their absence.

This shows that in schools surveyed, the performance were not good. Other students did not attend schools because of helping their families to find money so as to afford their lives by engaging in small businesses. Moreover, their families being poor, most students engaged in crimes such as theft in order to find some amount of money. This situation is in line with David's research when he states: "Poverty is an important factor accounting for differences in performance and achievement across rural and sub-urban districts. Along with parents' ability to educate their offspring, the economic status of people plays a huge role in their own education."[29] Moreover, Egunsola, in his study among students at Adamawa State in Nigeria to determine the effect of home environment to academic performance, found that parental education and parental economic status had a considerable correlation to students' poor academic performance.[30] Therefore, these studies support that there is a great relationship between the poverty of families and students' poor performance in their studies. David further observes that "learners from low socio-economic status families tend to value domestic activities more than schooling. Such children are subjected to child labor and have a little time for studies."[31]

According to the results obtained, some students also mentioned sickness as one of the causes of absenteeism, whereby about 33.3% of students mentioned this. Students failed to attend in class because of sickness of various diseases which caused them miss some of the studies which hindered them from performing well in their studies, hence poor performance. Therefore, students' sickness was one of the factors which led to students' poor academic performance. These results are in line with the *Basic Education*

---

29. David, "Determinants of Poor Academic performance," 48.

30. Egunsola, "Influence of Home Environment," 28, cf. Clement, "Factors influencing the Academic Performance"; Magati, Bosire & Ogeta, "Factors affecting Academic Performance."

31. David, "Determinants of Poor Academic Performance.

CURRENT STATE OF ACADEMIC PERFORMANCE

Statistics Report of 2009/10 which states that the most common reason for absenteeism of students in schools is illness followed by deaths occurring in families. Indeed, illness is a recurring factor which contributes strongly to absenteeism, dropout and non-enrolment.

Influences from Peer-groups

This study also found out that the existence of peer groups was one of the causes of students' absenteeism. About 17.8% of teachers mentioned peer groups as one of the causes of students' absenteeism. This means that students engaged with groups which were not good for encouraging them to study hard or engaged with groups of people who were not studying. This engagement to inappropriate groups caused them to hate studies and not attend school; hence, this absence caused poor performance in their studies. These findings suggest that there is a strong relationship between truancy and the amounts of unsupervised time that truants spend with peers. Additionally, David notes: "Truancy can start early and is associated with poor academic achievement both in the short term and in later years. The chronic absence in schools has immediate consequences for academic performance in first grade.... Additionally, the majority of students who suffer from chronic absence come from families who do not possess the resources to help the children make up for lost learning. These early patterns have long-term costs for both the individual and society at large...."[32]

In his study at Sumbawanga Region, David found that truancy was also caused by the notion of scarce job opportunities in the country. Most truants had the notion that there are few job vacancies in private and public sectors, and that there was no need for them to study hard because most people who completed

---

32. David, "Determinants of Poor Academic Performance," 24; cf. Clement, "Factors Influencing the Academic Performance"; Magati, Bosire & Ogeta, "Factors affecting Academic Performance"; Olalekan, "Influence of Peer Group Relationship"; Temitope & Christy, "Influence of Peer Group on Academic Performance"; Liu, "Peer Group Effects on Students Outcomes."

secondary education were roaming around without jobs. In the interview, one of his respondents said: *"There is no need of wasting time at school because numerous secondary graduates are roaming around without a recognized job employment either from public or non-public sector in rural and urban areas respectively."*[33] The above statement indicates the false hope that most truants had in his study area; and this is the same hope that most truants have in other secondary schools which make them despise studying and value other activities like casual labors, drugs, etc., instead of education leading them to poor academic performance. It is probably true that vacancies for employed jobs are scarce in private and public sectors. However, the notion of truants goes against the meaning and aims of education. It ascribes education only to the narrow scope of mere employment. Though employment is important, acquiring education hardly means that all people should be employed by private and public sectors. Education enables those who acquire it have a broad spectrum of how to manage life, including having the ability to compete to the available scarce job vacancies.

Other Factors which Cause Students' Absenteeism

There are other factors which were mentioned by students in the three selected schools which caused students' absenteeism; and these also affected students' academic performance, which included: fear of students to their teachers, students' dislike of some of the subjects, students' bad behavior, hunger, tiredness, distance from home to school, presentations, students not fulfilling exercises, relationship, escaping exercises, as well as coming late to school. These factors caused students' absenteeism; and consequently affected their academic performance.[34]

From the above factors, which cause students' absenteeism, there is a need for teachers to establish favorable environments for

33. Ibid., 45; cf. Olalekan, "Influence of Peer Group Relationship"; Temitope & Christy, "Influence of Peer Group on Academic Performance"; Liu, "Peer Group Effects on Students Outcomes."

34. Cf. Magati, Bosire & Ogeta, "Factors affecting Academic Performance."

CURRENT STATE OF ACADEMIC PERFORMANCE

their students so as to avoid students' fear from them. On their part, students are required to be serious with their studies by observing all school rules as well as doing all academic issues directed by their teachers. Despite the above factors mentioned by students from the selected schools, there are other factors which may cause students' absenteeism such as child labor, lack of encouragements from parents and teachers, too much freedom given to students by their parents and shortage of school facilities which require utmost attention to enhance students' better academic performance.

Academic Challenges to Teachers and Students

After discussing the other factors that cause absenteeism and poor academic performance in the above sub-section, this section discusses some of the challenges facing teachers and students in the teaching and learning process—the shortage of teaching and learning facilities, the shortage of teachers to facilitate students' learning, especially in science subjects, and unfavorable teaching and learning environments.

Shortage of Teaching and Learning Facilities

During this study, it was found out that in most Community Secondary Schools, there was a shortage of enough facilities such as science and arts books, laboratory equipment which indicated that this was one of the challenges which contributed to students' poor performance, especially in national form four examination results. About 33.3% of teachers mentioned the shortage of teaching facilities as being the factor contributing to students' poor academic performance in Community Secondary Schools. And about 66.6% of students also mentioned the shortage of learning facilities as a factor or challenge which they faced and affected their performance.

A similar result is reported by David in his study at Sumbawanga District, Rukwa Region. In his question to one of the teachers who was teaching Physics subject in one of the surveyed schools as to why he demonstrated the Archimedes Principle in class and not in the laboratory, the teacher replied: "You know, there is no any laboratory infrastructure existing at our school since it was opened more than eight years ago. He went further by saying that all science national form four examinations are alternative to practical instead of being performed practically."[35]

David's finding above shows that the shortage of teaching and learning facilities is one of the greatest factors contributing to students' poor academic performance. These learning facilities are the ones which support greatly the process of teaching and learning, such as presence of books, and laboratory equipment. David's finding is in line with Altbach who points out that, there is a problem of textbooks in developing countries' schools where in many cases students either lack textbooks or are forced to share a few available textbooks.[36] David's and Altbach's above findings highlight for the need to increase equipment in laboratories for teaching science subjects and discouraging what is called "alternative to practical" which leaves students out of reality. To our opinion, alternative to practical in ordinary level education in Tanzanian schools leaves a gap of knowledge to students when they move to advanced level education. Hence, there is no continuation between the alternatives in ordinary level and the real practical works they have to do in advanced level and tertiary education. We would rather opine that practical works be done in all levels from primary to tertiary education because science without practical work is not science but just memorizations of facts. Learning by doing fosters students' curiosity and an interest in the respective subject, hence affecting students positively towards academic performance.

---

35. David, "Determinants of Poor Academic Performance," 57; cf. Clement, "Factors Influencing the Academic Performance"; Magati, Bosire & Ogeta, "Factors affecting Academic Performance."

36. Altbach, "Key Issues of Textbook Provision."

CURRENT STATE OF ACADEMIC PERFORMANCE

Shortage of Teachers, especially Science Teachers

The quality of education of any learning institution depends solely on the quality of teachers who impart knowledge to students and facilitate students' own learning. Teachers are pillars in the teaching and learning because they hold the curriculum of the institution in their hands and enable ambitious students achieve their academic anticipated goals. Shortage of competent teachers shatters the ambitions of students in institutions and the educational ambition of the institutions and the nation as a whole. In his research on the way heads of schools struggled to alleviate the problem of shortage of teachers to Community Secondary Schools in Bukoba Municipality, Kagera Region in Tanzania, Projest found out that most school administrators used form six leavers, part time teachers and teachers from remedial classes in order to ensure the implementation of the subject curricular.[37] In addition, Lymo, Too, and Kipng'etich conducted a study to assess the adequacy of teaching staff to Community Secondary Schools in Arusha District in Tanzania. Their findings indicated that schools had few teachers who were obliged to take heavy loads of teaching which hindered their effective teaching.[38] The use of unqualified teaching staff just for the sake of accomplishing the requirement of the curricular is not only dangerous to the respective students being taught, but also to the nation as a whole because of the incompetent graduates produced by incompetent teachers.

Similarly, most students in our surveyed schools indicated that the shortage of teachers especially science teachers was one of the great challenges which affected their academic performance. Where the number of teachers available did not satisfy the number of students available, mostly in Community Secondary Schools, the number of science teachers was not enough to students

---

37. Projest, "The effect of Shortage of Teachers."

38. Lymo, Too, and Kipng'etich, "Assessment of Teaching Staff," cf. Subair & Talabi, "Teacher Shortage"; Beytekin & Chipala, "The Quality Standardization"; Alami, "Causes of Poor Academic Performance."

available; there were schools which had only one science teacher with the number of students more than eighty hundred!

In the surveyed schools, about 64.4% of students mentioned the shortage of teachers for science subjects as one of the big challenges which hindered their academic performance. However, there were other students who agreed and others disagreed on the number of teachers to be enough and corresponded to the number of students. About 24.4% agreed that in their schools teachers were enough and corresponded to students available, and about 75.6% of students disagreed that in their schools the number of teachers was not enough and did not correspond to the available number of students. The findings are shown in the table below.

Table 20: Is the Number of Teachers enough and Correspond to the Number of Students?

	Frequency	Percent
Yes	11	24.4
No	34	75.6
Total	45	100.0

Source: Field Data, May–June 2017

In most Community Secondary Schools, it was observed that there was a small number of teachers as compared to the number of students available. There are a number of factors causing this small number of teachers such as poor school environment, as well as the government not employing enough number of teachers in most Community Secondary Schools. These factors relate to David's research in Sumbawanga District. When he asked one teacher at one of the surveyed schools about his leaving and working conditions, the teacher responded with a deep feeling: "*Look at these houses which do not have access of electrical energy made my computer being useless in this era of globalization for high development of sciences and technology.... [T]he monthly salary that I get is not adequate to purchase monthly basic needs and have a surplus to purchase a generator which is also very costly to run by filing fuel which is at high price in rural areas. The lack of electricity service gives a hard time for lesson preparation and in marking students' exercises or tests in the night.*"[39]

Following the above response David asserts that: "The few teachers in the government payrolls are poorly remunerated as a result most of them take up part time employment or private business enterprise in order to make ends meet."[40] He further notes, "the problems of poor working conditions to teachers result in higher absenteeism, reduced levels of effort, and lower effectiveness in the classroom, low morale, and reduced job satisfaction. Where working conditions are good, they result in enthusiasm, high morale, cooperation, and acceptance of responsibility. Teachers have been shown to have an important influence on students' academic achievement."[41] In his research to the district authorities, David had the following results:

> "the District Secondary Education Officer reported that the District Council had a need of 507 qualified teachers in the year of 2011/12. But, only 279 (55%) teachers were available in secondary schools found in Sumbawanga District. The deficit of teachers in the district was about 228 (45%) of qualified teachers. It was also reported that 58 (11.44%) of untrained teachers were hired to supplement teachers' deficit prevailing in the district. Out of 58 teachers, only 11 (19%) of untrained teachers were females and 47 (81%) were male teachers. The teacher student's ratio in the district was 1:36."[42]

These data show that there is a great relationship between the number of teachers available and students' academic performance. They also point to the need for the government to create conducive environments in Community Secondary Schools so as to increase

---

39. David, "Determinants of Poor Academic performance," 63; cf. Clement, "Factors influencing the Academic Performance"; Magati, Bosire & Ogeta, "Factors affecting Academic Performance."
40. Ibid., 35.
41. Ibid.
42. Ibid., 61.

teachers' morality and reduce their absenteeism, which will most likely help to increase students' academic performance.

Moreover, it was observed from this study that there was a larger number of arts subjects teachers than the number of science subjects teachers according to the data collected from a sample of teachers as shown in the table below.

Table 21: Number of Teachers per Subject

Subject	X Secondary Shool	Y Secondary School	Z Secondary School
Geography	5	2	1
Physics		1	
Chemistry		1	1
Biology		2	1
Math	1	1	
History	5	2	1
Civics	1	3	1
Commerce			2
Bookkeeping			1
English	3	3	2
Kiswahili	2	1	1

Source: Field Data, May–June 2017

The presented data in the table above are in line with David's study in Sumbawanga. David states thus in regard to the status of teachers in one of his surveyed schools:

> "Mzindakaya secondary school had an ordinary level ('O' level) education programs. The findings from this school revealed that; 13 (44.83%) teachers were available, in which 9 teachers were males whose qualifications were; 2 degree holders in sciences, and 5 degree holders in Arts. In addition to that, one teacher was diploma holder in sciences and 61 another one diploma holder in arts respectively. Also 4 teachers were females; in which 2 of them were Degree and 2 Diploma holders in arts

CURRENT STATE OF ACADEMIC PERFORMANCE

respectively. The teacher students' ratio was noted to be 1:45 at this school. It was reported that; the deficit of teachers prevailing at this school was about 55%."[43]

The distribution of teachers from the table above and that of David's research show that there is a need for the government to increase the number of qualified teachers especially for science subjects so as to cope with the number of available students in most Community Secondary Schools. In addition, these results show that the number of scientists in the future will be lower especially in Community Secondary Schools. Therefore, more efforts are required to train science students so as to increase the number of scientists in the country by increasing the number of science teachers.

Unfavorable Teaching and Learning Environments

Environments include the surrounding which the person finds oneself in. School environment are the school surroundings which the student finds oneself in. In this study, about 31.1% of students mentioned environments as another challenge which faced them and had negative impact in their performance and the remaining percent did not mention environments as the challenge to their academic performance. And about 29.6% of teachers mentioned environment as one of the factors which affected their teaching process which also would affect students' academic performance because there was no availability of enough teaching and learning facilities like books, libraries and laboratory equipment.

Environment is one of the factors which may encourage students to learn effectively and comfortably. Similar findings as those obtained from our field study were reported by Egunsola who revealed that conditions or environments of the school affect students' academic performance.[44] Moreover, Kaguo reports

43. Ibid.
44. Egunsola, "Influence of Home Environment"; cf. Jovinius, "An Investigation of the Geographical Location"; Chukwuemeka, "Environmental influence on Academic performance"; Clement, "Factors influencing the

that the presence of well-furnished and adequate dormitories or hostels and enough toilets offer favorable conditions for teaching and learning process; hence students' academic performance in the schools. The school learning environment as an input must be conducive to facilitate students' learning, hence good performance.[45] Therefore, there is a need to improve learning and teaching environments to both teachers and students which attracts them to learn and study comfortably, hence attain better performance.

Lack of Study Seriousness to Students

Students' malingering habit and procrastination are some of the great causes of failure in their examinations. Nakalema and Ssenyonga state:

> Study habits are strategies and methods of purposeful learning, usually centered on reading and writing. Effective study skills are essential for students to acquire good grades in school, and are useful in general to improve learning throughout one's life, in support of career and other interests.... Study habits include skills that enable a learner to systematically plan, access, record, organize, encode, and use information on their own in order to achieve a certain goal.... Time management, setting realist academic targets, setting rewards for completion of a task, revision, note taking, and organization of materials are critical study habits that have an impact on a learner's academic performance....[46]

Nakalema and Ssenyonga conclude thus: "Life at the university [or any other academic environment] involves juggling many

---

Academic Performance"; Magati, Bosire & Ogeta, "Factors affecting Academic Performance."

45. Kaguo, "Factors Influencing Academic Performance."
46. Nakalema & Sseyonga, "Academic Stress," 5; cf. Benwari & Nemine, "Intensive Reading"; Owusu-Acheaw, "Reading Habits"; Helsel & Miles, "Assessment of Student Study Habit"; Clement, "Factors Influencing the Academic Performance", Magati, Bosire & Ogeta, "Factors affecting Academic Performance."

CURRENT STATE OF ACADEMIC PERFORMANCE

things like reading books and chapters, meeting paper/coursework deadlines, and participating in the usual university extracurricular activities making the students feel like there is not enough time to complete all their work adequately . . . ."[47] In this kind of life, academic procrastination and laziness have no place to effective students.

What university students are facing, as described by Nakalema and Ssenyonga above is quite similar to students in other levels of study including the secondary level education. However, this study also found out that there was a problem to students studying habit; they were not serious with their studies, which was one of the factors that caused them attain poor academic performance in their examinations. About 29.6% of teachers mentioned lack of seriousness to students as the factor which contributed to students' poor academic performance and about 20% of students also mentioned students' laziness and lack of awareness as the challenge that faced and affected their academic performance. Lack of seriousness in studying led most of them to academic procrastination.[48] Therefore, their studying habit, contrary to what was required of a student, was another main determinant of their poor academic performance.

Poor Cooperation among Educational Stakeholders

This was one of the factors mentioned by both teachers and students that affected students' performance. They said that there is no cooperation between students themselves which made them being together and cooperate in their studies. Furthermore, there was no cooperation between students and their teachers caused by some of the teachers being harsh to their students causing students' fear from their teacher and sometimes hate their subjects. This teachers' attitude caused negative effects on academic

---

47. Ibid.
48. Cf. Alami, "Causes of Poor Academic Performance"; Solomon & Rothblum, "Academic Procrastination"; Brownlow & Reasinger, "Putting off Until Tomorrow."

performance to their students. There was no cooperation between teachers and parents, whereby parents did not make any follow up on the academic progress of their children. This brought difficulties to teachers in taking care of children due to lack of support from parents. About 17.7% of students mentioned cooperation between students and teachers being low and about of 7.4% of teachers mentioned cooperation between parents and teachers being low. The results indicate that the disintegration between the parts can hardly enhance the organism to function properly as advocated by the theory of organization discussed in chapter two above.

Due to these results, there is a need for the school administration to educate parents to establish strong relationships with parents; moreover parents are required to take care of their children and sometimes encourage them to study hard by providing them motivations, supporting much in educational issues and making follow ups of students' studies. This inward motivation helps students to study hard and love school.

One question was asked to the heads of schools about the responses of parents on educational issues; whether it was positive or negative. About 100% of the heads of schools indicated that there was negative relationship between parents and educational issues as shown in the table below.

Table 22: Parents' Responses on Educational Issues

Response	Frequency	Percent
Positive	-	-
Negative	3	100.0

Source: Field Data, May–June 2017

We agree that there is poor cooperation among students and their parents, and a poor cooperation between students and their teachers and teachers and parents as indicated in the discussion above. This is because most of the parents do not have enough education about the importance of education to their children and their contribution, as parents, on various education issues, which is one of the important factors to help in increasing students' academic performance. This is clearly stated by David as follows: "The home environment also affects the academic performance of students. Educated parents can provide such an environment that suits best for academic success of their children. . . . [T] the academic performance of students heavily depends upon the parental involvement in their academic activities to attain the higher level of quality in academic success. . . ."[49]

Following this factor, there is a need for school administrations to put more efforts on educating parents on the importance of creating conducive environments to students even making follow-ups in their studies so as to make them perform better in their studies. Marzano, points out that the school authorities can provide counseling and guidance to parents for creating positive home environment for improvement in students' quality of work.[50] Therefore, improving environments for teaching and learning process most likely helps to increase students, performance in Community Secondary Schools.

Students' Truant Behavior

Truancy was another problem that caused massive failures in academic performance in the researched schools. The study findings show that about 89.9% of students indicated that there was the problem of truancy in their schools, and about 11.1% of students ignored that there was no problem of truancy in their schools. These results show that there is a great relationship between the problem of truancy and students' performance. The results are shown in the table below.

---

[49]. David, Determinants of Poor Academic Performance," 27; cf. Alami, "Causes of Poor Academic Performance"; Farooq, Chaudhry, Shafiq & Berhanu, "Factors Affecting Students' Quality" 6; Clement, "Factors Influencing the Academic Performance"; Magati, Bosire & Ogeta, "Factors Affecting Academic Performance."

[50]. Marzano, *What Works in Schools?*

Table 23: Is Truancy one of the Problems in Your School?

	Frequency	Percent
Yes	40	88.9
No	5	11.1
Total	45	100.0

Source: Field Data, May–June 2017

Moreover, about 33.3% of teachers mentioned the problem of truancy as one of the factors contributing to students' poor performance. There were many other factors which caused students' absenteeism such as some students coming from poor families where they could not afford uniform, different school needs, and sicknesses.

In addition, there were about 40.7% of teachers who concluded that students' attendance was moderate, and about 40.7% others concluded that students' attendance was good and about 22.2% concluded that students' attendance was poor. These results indicate that there was a problem of absenteeism or truancy to some extent which was one of the factors contributing to students' poor performance in Community Secondary Schools. A similar study by Titilayo investigated the impact of truancy and absenteeism to secondary school students in Ogun State in Nigeria. The study indicated that unmonitored children were very much in the danger of acquiring abnormal behavior in their school attendance leading to failures in examinations.[51] David also notes that despite causing law performance among students, truancy and absenteeism increase the rates of drug uses among students. According to him, this increase is caused by the long time which truants stay with their peers without the supervision of their teachers.[52]

---

51. Titiliyo, "Abseteeism and Truancy," cf. Nakalema & Ssenyonga, "Academic Stress"; Odumbe, Simatwa & Ayodo, "Factors Influencing Student Academic Performance"; Ayodele, "Class Attendance"; Clement, "Factors Influencing the Academic Performance"; Magati, Bosire & Ogeta, "Factors affecting Academic Performance"; Oluremi, "Truancy and Academic Performance"; Mapesa, Peer Influence on Academic Performance."

52. David, "Determinants of Poor Academic Performance," 25; cf. Oluremi,

CURRENT STATE OF ACADEMIC PERFORMANCE

There is a need to address this problem by removing all problems which may cause students' absenteeism, for example building school walls, having enough teachers who will cover all periods which will cover the chance of students to be loose and long to be out of school, educating students on the impact of engaging with bad groups, and removing punishments and harsh treatments so as to encourage them to enter in classes regularly. Chang and Romero state that the majority of students who suffer from chronic absence come from families which do not possess resources to help children make up for lost learning. These early patterns have long-term costs for both the individual and society at large. Moreover, being absent from class decreases the student's ability to learn, which will eventually contribute to students' attaining poor academic performance.[53] All these assertions indicate the great potential which truancy has towards students' failures in their studies, and which need to be counteracted for students' better academic performance.

Other Factors affecting Students' Performance

Despite the factors discussed above, there are other factors which contribute to students' poor academic performance from both teachers and students. These factors include the following: love issues, fear from teachers, school rules, distance from home to school, students not understanding what was taught by their teachers, homework, exercises, workload to teachers, poor parental care to their children, shortage of classrooms, hunger, government policy not favoring teachers, teachers not updating their knowledge and teachers not being motivated. Moreover, Lepp, Barkley & Karpinski and Kibona and Mgaya found in their studies that the rate of decrease in academic performance among students in higher learning institutions were directly proportional to the use of phones among students. Students spend more time to chart,

---

"Truancy and Academic Performance"; Mapesa, Peer Influence on Academic Performance."

53. Chang & Romero, "Present, Engaged and Accounted for."

Facebook, WhatsApp and Twitter communications with peers and friends more than they spent time in studying subject materials leading them to academic procrastination. The transfers of teachers from one school to another voluntarily or involuntarily affect students' academic performances.[54] From the factors mentioned by students and by the above scholars as the ones contributing to students' poor performance, there is a need for the government and the school administration to increase the number of classrooms to reduce overcrowding of students in one stream which makes it easy for students to understand what is taught by their teachers. Moreover, parents should take much care of their children. Moreover, in-service training motivations are needed to teachers to help them in updating their knowledge.

Conclusion

The main concern of this chapter was to present and discuss the findings about the factors which contribute to students' poor academic performance in Community Secondary Schools at the surveyed area. A large number of respondents indicated that environments were not conducive to learning and teaching; facilities were not enough and did not match with the number of students available; the general academic performance was moderate; and there was a problem of absenteeism which contributed to students' poor academic performance. Therefore this situation calls for more effort to ensure students perform better especially in National examination results by working effectively with those factors contributing to students' poor performance.

---

54. Lepp, Barkley & Karpinski "The Relationship between Cell Phone Use and Academic Performance" and Kibona and Mgaya, "Smartphone's effects on Academic Performance"; cf. Kirschner & Karpinski, "Facebook and Academic Performance"; Lee, et al., "Smartphone Addiction"; Rubin & Nutter-Upham, "Academic Procrastination"; Reynolds, "Factors affecting Academic Procrastination"; Schraw & Wadkins, "Doing the Things We Do"; Solomon & Rothblum, "Academic Procrastination"; Brownlow & Reasinger, "Putting off unitl Tomorrow."

CURRENT STATE OF ACADEMIC PERFORMANCE

This chapter has revealed that there were various factors which contributed or influenced students' performance. These factors include: learning and teaching environments, and teaching and learning facilities. If these factors were considered effectively it would be easy for students to perform well and teachers do their work effectively. Therefore, these factors called for the need to all Community Secondary Schools to ensure there were enough teaching and learning materials and favorable teaching and learning environments to both teachers and students.

Moreover, the findings in this chapter reveal that there is a shortage of teaching and learning facilities, poor teaching and learning environments, poor cooperation among the students, between parents and teachers, lack of students' seriousness in studies as factors contributing to students' poor academic performance in most Community Secondary Schools.

This chapter has also indicated that there are many factors mentioned by students about the causes of absenteeism, which include poverty, sickness, punishment, harsh treatments from their teachers, peer groups. Other factors included presentations, students' fear of their teachers, the distance from home to school, and coming late to school. These factors caused students' poor performance and called for the need of school administration to address on all these causes to ensure better performance of their students. Generally, all the factors discussed in this chapter call for the need of the government and school administrations to put more efforts in addressing on these factors so as to ensure better performance in Community Secondary Schools. It is on the basis of the findings discussed above that we provide our recommendations in the following chapter.

Chapter 5

TOWARDS THE FUTURE OF COMMUNITY SECONDARY SCHOOLS IN TANZANIA

Introduction

IN THIS CHAPTER, THE study summarizes the main findings and issues. The main issues in this book were investigating the factors which contributed to students' poor performance in Community Secondary Schools in Tanzania, and examining the challenges and future prospects of these schools. The chapter provides the conclusions and recommendations for action and areas of further research. Therefore, this chapter includes our opinions which will possibly be useful for most Community Secondary Schools to overcome the problem of students' poor academic performance and enhance better performance in their studies.

Summary of Study Findings

As also highlighted in the conclusion of the previous chapter, the results obtained from this study correspond with the literatures surveyed and the theoretical perspectives guiding the study. The results show that most Community Secondary Schools in Tanzania experience poor performance in their examinations, especially the form four national examination results. The students' poor performance in Community Secondary Schools is mainly caused by a number of factors as it has been mention by teachers and students from the surveyed Community Secondary Schools such as shortage of teachers especially science teachers, shortage of facilities such as books especially (science books, laboratory equipment), environments not being conducive for both teachers and students for teaching and learning process, lack of motivation to teachers, truancy, punishment and harsh treatment to students by their teachers, poor cooperation between students, teachers and parents. All these factors lead to poor students' performance in their studies. Moreover, the results obtained from this study show that most Community Secondary Schools lack enough teachers of science subjects as was mentioned by a number of students that in their schools there was no enough science teachers as compared to teachers of arts subjects. Since most studies conducted in other parts of Tanzania used in this book indicate similar results, it can be concluded that most Community Secondary Schools in Tanzania suffer from poor academic performance, hence jeopardizing the national education plans and the preparation of future work force. This poor academic performance calls for immediate actions to ensure better provision of education in these schools.

Future Prospects of Community Secondary Schools

What should be done in order to ensure better provision of education in Community Secondary Schools in Tanzania? Basing on the findings of this study highlighted above, this study provides the following working recommendations for the nourishment of students' academic performance in Community Secondary Schools: first, there should be an improvement in primary education. There are some students entering secondary education without knowing how to write and read properly making it difficult for them to understand their studies well, and becoming difficult to teachers to teach them; more efforts are needed to make students be able to read and write properly in primary schools. Since the language of instruction in most Tanzanian primary schools is Kiswahili and English is taught as a subject, and the language of instruction (LoI) in secondary schools is English, the efforts should also be directed towards an adequate teaching of English language at this level. Otherwise, the change of the LoI from English to Kiswahili could be a better option.[1]

Second, in-service training should be provided to teachers so as to update their knowledge, this also is one of the important measures to be taken by educational officers because most teachers are not up to date with the syllabus to be used when they are teaching; some of them still use materials which are for many years past. Teachers should also be encouraged to be students throughout their lives. They should be encouraged to update their teaching notes and encourage student-centered teaching methods. Teachers need to update themselves because education is not static; it is always current and changing.

Third, there should be rights to teachers to participate in making and implementing educational policies because these are the ones who know about the needs of students and are the ones who face many challenges during the teaching process. According to Nyangosia's research discussed in chapter two above, one of the instructional strategies which schools at Nyeri and Kiambu in Kenya use in order to ensure effective teaching was involving teachers in the decisions of issues regarding the best strategies to improve teaching. Involving teachers made schools in Nyeri and Kiambu succeed in implementing their planned curricular.[2] Therefore, there should be an active involvement of teachers in formulating policies on educational issues.

Fourth, there should be an active participation of parents on various educational issues when school administrations are in need of supports from them. Moreover, education is required by

---

1. Cf. Mligo & Mwashilindi, English *as a Language of Teaching and Learning*.

2. Nyangosia, "Determinants of Differential Kenya Certificate of Secondary Education."

TOWARDS THE FUTURE

parents about the importance of their contribution in increasing students' performance by caring for their children in issues relating to education and making follow ups on the academic progress of their children. This is important because children take advantage of the ignorance of their parents to not take their studies seriously. Therefore, we would argue here that there is a possible relationship between students' academic procrastination and the home parenting of children which parents have to address.

Fifth, efforts should be made to improve the use of English language to students in Community Secondary Schools because they fail their examinations mostly because of their failure to explain themselves in English.[3] The question of language of instruction is a serious one. Most students, especially those from Community Secondary Schools located in rural areas speak their vernaculars code-mixing with Kiswahili language instead of English in school environments. David in his research among the Fipa of Rukwa Region found that most students spoke Fipa language mixing it with Kiswahili because most of them belonged to the Fipa tribe. He reports the response of one of his interviewee: *"It is very obvious that Kifipa is spoken at large by most students mixing with Kiswahili and English is spoken mainly during class sessions. He clarified by insisting that most of the students are selected from the primary schools located in the same ward whose habitants are Fipa ethnic group."*[4] Another response added: *"Incompetence of English language contributed to students' poor academic performance because the chances of competency spirit that could be instigated by students from other regions was limited due to ward wise selection criteria of students that restrict them to be enrolled in secondary within their ward."*[5] This means that there is a need for improving English language used in academic arenas for secondary and tertiary education and remove an obligation to recruit students for Community Secondary Schools from within the Ward as it perpetuates tribalism among students. However, improvement of English

---

3. Mligo & Mwashilindi, *English as a Language of Teaching and Learning*.
4. David, "Determinants of Poor Academic Performance," 46.
5. Ibid.

proficiency can hardly be possible without involving first language speakers who studied English in their respective countries. The English language proficiency issue indicates the need to engage English language experts in teaching teachers at teachers' colleges for teachers and English language experts for teaching English at secondary schools.

Sixth, there should be competitions in Community Secondary Schools as done in some private secondary schools. Competitions should be well-planned and motivating to both teachers and their respective students. Regular competition will make them anxious to have better examination results which in turn will encourage students to study hard so as to be first in their examinations.

Seventh, there is a need to improve environments to both teachers and students by ensuring that the environments surrounding schools are conducive and encourage students to learn and teachers to teach. Issues such as the availability of books, laboratory equipment, enough classrooms filled with windows and doors, impressive school walls are necessary for students so as to discourage them from absenteeism. Teaching environments are one of the motivating factors for teachers to teach and students to study hard.

Eighth, the government should provide enough facilities and teachers by ensuring every Community Secondary School has enough facilities and teachers which match with the number of students available in such schools. It should be taken into account that there can hardly be a school without students and teachers. The adequate number of teachers in a particular Community Secondary School is needed in order for effective teaching and learning to take place. Since most Community Secondary Schools are under the mentorship of the government, it is responsible to make sure that enough teachers are allocated to these schools.

Ninth, schools should provide examinations frequently, introduce remedial classes, clubs and exercises to students and reduce the number of students in classrooms for easy class management. All these are part and parcel of students' practices. Always practice makes perfect. Since students are provided with the opportunity to practice, it is hoped that their performance will gradually change to the better.

Tenth, punishments should be reduced so as to reduce fear of students to their teachers, to reduce the problem of absenteeism which is one of the factors leading to students' poor academic performance. It has been noted from the above presentation and discussion of data that truancy and absenteeism are mainly caused by fear of students in regard to their teachers' harsh behaviors. However, it is not the opinion of this book to underscore the role of punishments as incentives to motivate students' learning process. Our opinion is that punishing students, and without following the guiding principles for punishing students, can cause them develop an environment of fear which can eventually be hostile to such students in their study process. Moreover, it is our opinion that intrinsic motivation strategies to students and teachers should be encouraged more than extrinsic ones.

Eleventh, students are required to change their study habits. They should be serious concentrating on their studies not on other affairs like engaging in romantic relationships. Romantic relationships, drug use, and laziness are enemies of academic performance. Moreover, they should avoid last minute cramming and memorizing for examinations which hardly help in raising their performance. Nakalema and Ssenyonga state: "Cramming when studying subject matter is one thing and the ability to remember the studied material is another.... Often students tend to use passive strategies when reading such as memorization with little emphasis on understanding main points of the information in order to only reproduce it on the upcoming examination...."[6] Hence, avoiding these activities and other related procrastinating habits is one of the ways of attaining good performance in their studies.

Twelfth, motivations and good salaries should be given to teachers so as to encourage them to do their work effectively. Students should intrinsically be encouraged to study hard. People who have been involved in teaching students in one way or another will agree that teaching involves thinking, time, and compassion

6. Nakalema & Sseyonga, "Academic Stress," 6.

of teachers to their learners. Since teaching is a self-giving of the teacher to his or her learners, it requires motivation and recognition. Motivation to teachers should be in terms of in time salary provision, performance motivations, in-service training and promotions.

Eventually, we would rather state that poor academic performance in the Tanzanian educational system is not limited to Community Secondary Schools investigated in this study. Other schools in the educational ladder can have different factors which contribute to their inadequate performance. It is therefore highly recommended that similar studies be conducted to investigate the factors contributing to students' poor academic performance in pre-primary, primary and tertiary education. Moreover, some studies can be conducted to other categories of secondary schools other than Community Secondary Schools (traditional government-built and private secondary schools) to determine the factors facing them. These researches may allow for comparison of the results of studies between different levels of education in Tanzania.

Conclusion

A large number of students in this study have shown that the environment prevailing in most Community Secondary Schools is not conducive making it difficult for them to attain better performance. Such environment include the lack of enough facilities for both teaching and learning to students, lack of cooperation among students, lack of adequate cooperation between teachers and parents which made it difficult for students to concentrate much in their studies, hence poor performance. It is our conviction that poor performance of students hampers the development of students individually and the nation as a whole because it hinders students who excel further for taking various roles in the future. To ensure better performance in Community Secondary Schools, more effort is required from the government (which is the one responsible in ensuring the improvement of Community Secondary Schools) and the school administration (who are the close supervisors of schools) towards the above stated recommendations. They are required to ensure that most necessary aspects supporting students' performance are well improved, are available, and correspond to the available number of students.

BIBLIOGRAPHY

Adediwura, A. and Tayo, B. "Perception of Teachers' Knowledge, Attitude and Teaching Skills as Predictor of Academic Performance in Nigerian Secondary Schools." *Educational Research and Review* 2:7 (2007) 165–171.

Adeyemi, T.O. "Teachers' teaching Experience and Students' Learning Outcomes in Secondary Schools in Ondo State, Nigeria." *Educational Research and Review* 3:6 (2008) 204–212.

Akiri, Agharuwhe A. "Effects of Teachers' Effectiveness on Students' Academic Performance in Public Secondary Schools; Delta State-Nigeria." *Journal of Educational and Social Research* 3:3 (2013) 105–111.

Alami, Manizheh. "Causes of Poor Academic Performance among Omani Students." *International Journal of Social Science Research* 4:1 (2016) 126–136.

Ayodele, Olufunmilayo D. "Class Attendance and Academic Performance of Second Year University Students in an Organic Chemistry Course." *African Journal of Chemical Education* 7:1 (2017) 63–75.

Arshad, Nadeem and Ahmed, Umair. "Impact of Breakfast Habits on Education Performance of University Students (A Study Conducted on University of Sargodha, Pakistan)." *International Journal of Academic Research in Progressive Education and Development* 3:1 (2014) 255–270.

Altbach, P. G. "Key issues of textbook provision in the third world prospects." *Journal of Prospect Education* 13:3 (1983) 125–132.

Barnard, W. M. "Parent Involvement in Elementary School and Educational Attainment." *Journal of Children and Youth Services Review* 26 (2004) 39–62.

Bascia, B. *Achieving Universal Primary Education by 2015: A Chance for every Child.* Washington, DC: World Bank, 2003.

Baranek, Lori Kay. "The Effect of Rewards and Motivation on Student Achievement." Masters of Education Theses. No. 285, 1996. http://scholarworks.gvsu.edu/theses/285.

Bell, J.M. "Definition of academic performance," 2014. Online at http://www.ehow.com/about_4740750_define-academic-performance.html (Accessed on 19th April, 2017.)

Benwari, Nnenna Ngozi & Nemine, Ebi- Bulami Bridget (2014). "Intensive Reading as a Study Habit and Students' Academic Achievement in

BIBLIOGRAPHY

Economics in Selected Secondary Schools in Bayelsa State, Nigeria." *Journal of Curriculum and Teaching* 3:2 (2014) 94–99.

Bertalanffy, L.V. "The History and Status of General Systems Theory." *The Academy of Management Journal* 15:4 (1972) 407–426.

Bertalanffy, L. V. *General Systems Theory: Foundations Development Applications*. New York, NY.: Braziller, 1969.

Beytekin, Osman Ferda and Chipala, HusseinCollins. "The Quality Standardization of Teachers in Malawi Government Secondary Schools." *British Journal of Education, Society & Behavioural Sciences* 11:1 (2015) 1–9.

Bourice, S. "How Small is Better? Relationship between class size: Teaching Practice and Students Achievement." *American Educational Research Journal* 4:6 (1986) 558–571.

Boma, A. "Factors Affecting Performance in Tanzania school." Dissertation for Award of M.A Degree, University of Dar es salaam, Tanzania, 1980.

Bloom, B. "Time and Learning." *Journal of American Psychologist* 29:4 (1974) 682–688.

Brock-Utne, Birgit and Desai, Zubeida. "Expressing Oneself through Writing—A Comparative Study of Learners' Writing Skills in Tanzania and South Africa." In *Language of Instruction in Tanzania and South Africa–Highlights from a Project*. Edited by Birgit Brock-Utne, Zubeida Desai, Martha A.S. Qorro and Allan Pitman, 11–31. Rotterdam: Sense, 2010.

Brock-Utne, Birgit and Holmarsdottir, Halla B. "Language Policies and Practices in Tanzania and South Africa: Problems and Challenges." *HakiElimu, Working Papers Series*. Dar es Salaam, 2005.

Brownlow, Sheila and Reasinger, Renee D. "Putting off until Tomorrow What is better done Today: Academic Procrastination as a Function of Motivation towards College Work." Ferrari, J.R. & Psychyl, T.A. (eds.). Procrastination: Current Issues and New Directions. *Journal of Social Behavior and Personality* 15:5 (2000) 15–34.

Corcoran, T. B., Walker, L. J. and White, J. L. *Working in Urban Schools*. Washington DC.: Institute for Educational Leadership, 1988.

Chang, H. N. and Romero M. "Present, Engaged and Accounted for: The Critical Importance of Addressing Chronic Absence in the Early Grade Report." *National Center for Children in Poverty*, Mailman University of Public Health, Columbia University, 2008, 1–31.

Chonjo, P.N. "The Quality of Education in Tanzania Schools: Assessment of Physical Facilities and Teaching Learning Materials." *Utafiti* 1:1 (1994) 36–46.

Chukwuemeka, Orlu. Environmental Influence on Academic Performance of Secondary School Students in Port Harcourt Local Government Area of Rivers State." *Journal of Economics and Sustainable Development* 4:12 (2013) 34–38.

BIBLIOGRAPHY

Clement, Isiye Muyabila. "Factors Influencing the Academic Performance of Day Scholars in Public Secondary Schools in Kenya: A Case of Mumias West Sub-County." Master of Arts Thesis, Project Planning and Management, University of Nairobi, Kenya, 2015.

David, Nyandwi Melack. "Determinants of Poor Academic Performance of Secondary School Students in Sumbawanga District, Tanzania." M.A Thesis in Rural Development. Sokoine University of Agriculture, Morogoro Tanzania, 2014.

Dial, Jaime C. "The Effect of Teacher Experience and Teacher Degree Levels on Student Achievement in Mathematics and Communication Arts." Doctor of Education Thesis. School of Education, Baker University, 2008.

Egunsola, A.O.E. "Influence of Home Environment on Academic Performance of Secondary School Students in Agricultural Science in Adamawa State Nigeria." *IOSR Journal of Research & Method in Education* 4:4 (2014) 46–53.

Ehiane, Stanley O. "Discipline and Academic Performance (A Study of Selected Secondary Schools in Lagos Nigeria)." *International Journal of Academic Research in Progressive Education and Development* 3:1 (2014) 181–194.

Elibariki, Nafikahedi. "Factors influencing Shortage of Teaching-learning Resources in Tanzania Primary Schools: A Case of Primary Schools in Kinondoni Municipality." Master of Education in Education Administration, Planning and Policy Studies, Dar es Salaam: The Open University of Tanzania, 2014.

Ebenuwa-Okoh, E.E. "Influence of Age, Financial Status, and Gender on Academic Performance among Undergraduates." *Journal of Psychology* 1:2 (2010) 99–103.

Ewetan, Temitope Oluwakemi and Ewetan, Olabanji Olukayode. "Teachers' Teaching Experience and Academic Performance in Mathematics and English Language in Public Secondary Schools in Ogun State, Nigeria." *International Journal of Humanities Social Sciences and Education* 2:2 (2015) 123–134.

Farooq, M.S, Chaudhry, A.H, Shafiq, M, & Berhanu, G. "Factors affecting Students' Quality of Academic Performance: A Case of Secondary School Level." *Journal of Quality and Technology Management* 7:2 (2011) 1–14.

Halou, Mammy M. and Caddy, Ian N. "Definition Problems and General Systems Theory Perspective in Supply Chain Management." *Problems and Perspectives in Management* 4:4 (2006) 77–83.

Hassan, Amour Haji and Bali, Theodora A.L. "Assessing the Effects of Corporal Punishment on Primary School Pupils' Academic Performance and Discipline in Unguja, Zanzibar." *International Journal of Education and Research* 1:12 (2013) 1–12.

Helsel, Diana G. and Miles, Randall J. Assessment of Student Study Habit Effects on Academic Performance in Introductory Agronomy Courses." *Journal of Agronomic Education* 14:2 (1985). 115–118.

BIBLIOGRAPHY

Iphofen, Ron. *Ethical Decision-Making in Social Research: A Practical Guide.* New York, NY.: Pelgrave Macmillan, 2009.

Invocavity, Josephine. "The effect of Corporal Punishment on Discipline among Students in Arusha Secondary Schools." Master of Education in Administration, Planning and Policy Studies. Dar es Salaam: Open University of Tanzania, 2014.

Israel, Mark and Hay, Ian. *Research Ethics for Social Scientists: Between Ethical Conduct and Regulatory Compliance.* London: Sage, 2006.

Jabor, M. Khata , Kungu, Kenneth, Machtmes, Krissana, Buntat, Yahya and Nordin, Mohd Safarin. "The Influence of Age and Gender on the Students' Achievement in Mathematics." *2011 International Conference on Social Science and Humanity* 5 (2011) 304–308.

Joseph, Adigun, John, Onihunwa , Eric, Ironukhai, Yusuf, Sada and Olbunmi, Adesina "Effect of Gender on Students' Academic Performance in Computer Studies in Secondary Schools in New Bussa, Borgu Local Government of Niger State." *Journal of Education and Practice* 6:33 (2015) 1–7.

Jovinus, Joseph. "An Investigation of the Effect of Geographical Location of Schools to the Students' Academic Performance: A Case of Public Secondary Schools in Muleba District." Master of Education Thesis. The Open University of Tanzania, 2015.

Kafyulilo, Ayoub Cherd. "Professional Development through Teacher Collaboration: An Approach to Enhance Teaching and Learning in Science and Mathematics in Tanzania." *Africa Education Review* 10:4 (2013) 671–688. Doi: 10.1080/18146627.2013.853560.

Kaguo, F.E. "Factors influencing Academic Performance of Students in Community and Government built Secondary Schools in Mbeya Municipality, Tanzania." Master of Science in Agricultural Education and Extension Thesis, Sokoine University of Agriculture. Morogoro, Tanzania, 2011.

Kibona, Lusekelo and Mgaya, Gervas. "Smartphones' Effects on Academic Performance of Higher Learning Students. A Case of Ruaha Catholic University–Iringa, Tanzania." *Journal of Multidisciplinary Engineering Science and Technology* 2:4 (2015) 777–784.

Kipkoech, B. K. "Influence of Socio-Economic Background on Academic Performance of Public Mixed Day Secondary School Students: A Case of Kuresoi District, Nakuru County." Master of Philosophy in Educational Psychology Thesis. Moi University, Eldoret, Kenya, 2012.

Kirschner, P.A. and Karpinski, A.C. "Facebook® and Academic Performance." *Computers in Human Behavior* 26 (2010) 1237–1245.

Komba, Ciril Kalembana, Hizza, Ernest Lucas and Jonathan, Winledy T.Y. "Factors influencing Academic Performance of Ward Secondary Schools: A Case of Selected Schools in Moshi Municipality and Moshi District, Tanzania." *Journal of Co-operative and Business Studies* 2:1 (2014) no page numbers.

BIBLIOGRAPHY

Kothari, C. R. *Research methodology, Methods and Techniques*. New Delhi: New International, 2009.

Lam, D. *Generating Extreme Inequality: Schooling, Earnings and Intergenerational Transmission of Human Capital in South Africa and Brazil*. Report No. 99-439. Ann. Arbor, Michigan: Population studies centre, University of Michigan, 1999.

Laddunuri, M.M. "Status of School Education in present Tanzania and Emerging Issues" *International Journal of Educational Research and Technology* 3 (2012) 15-20.

Lee, J., Cho, B., Kim, Y and Noh, J. "Smartphone Addiction in University Students and its Implication for Learning," in *Emerging Issues in Smart Learning*, ed: Springer (2015) 297-305.

Lepp, Andrew, Barkley1, Jacob E. and Karpinski, Aryn C. "The Relationship Between Cell Phone Use and Academic Performance in a Sample of U.S. College Students." *SAGE Open* (2015) 1-9.

Leuven, Edwin, Oosterbeek, Hessel and Klaauw, Bas van der. The Effect of Financial Rewards on Students' Achievement: Evidence from a Randomized Experiment." *Journal of the European Economic Association* 8:6 (2010) 1243-1265.

Liu, Keke. "Peer Group Effects on Students Outcomes: Evidence from Randomized Lotteries." Doctor of Philosophy Thesis. Vanderbilt University, Nashville, Tennessee, 2010.

Lyimo, Naisujaki Sephania, Too, Jackson K. and Kipng'etich, Kirui Joseph (2017). "Perception of Teachers on Availability of Instructional Materials and Physical Facilities in Secondary schools of Arusha District, Tanzania." *International Journal of Educational Policy Research and Review* 4:5 (2017). 103-112.

———. (2017). "Assessment of Teaching Staff Adequacy in Tanzanian Community Secondary Schools: A Case of Arusha District." *International Journal of Educational Policy Research and Review* 4:5 (2017) 81-89.

Lugayila, Erick Nyanda. "Assessment of Factors influencing Form Four Students' Examination Performance: A Case of Maswa District." Master Thesis in Education Administration, Planning and Policy Studies. Dar es Salaam: Open University of Tanzania, 2014.

Lupogo, Issaya. "The Intensity of Language of Instruction Problem in Tanzanian Universities: Is it a Numeracy and Literacy Background Case?" *Pyrex Journal of Educational Research and Reviews* 2 (2016) 48-54.

Magati, N. W, Bosire, K and Ogeta N. "Factors Affecting Academic Performance in day Secondary Schools in Borabu District in Kenya." *International Journal of Current Business and Social Sciences* 1:3 (2015) 19-31.

Mapesa, Misanya Sophy. "Peer Influence on Academic Performance of Form One Students in Girls Boarding Secondary Schools in Kanduyi Constituency: Kenya." Master of Arts in Project Planning and Management, The University of Nairobi, Kenya.

BIBLIOGRAPHY

Marzano, R. J. *What Works In Schools: Translating Research into Action?* 2003. [Online at: http://pdonline.ascd.org/pd_online/whatworks/marzano2003_ch13.html [Site visited on 15/06/2017].

Masatu, Samwel M.A. "Assessment of the Current Status of Students' Academic Performance in Science Subjects in Relation to the Initiatives implemented in Secondary Schools in Tanzania." Master of Science in Human Resource Management Thesis, Mzumbe University, Morogoro Tanzania, 2013.

Mkalangale, Vumbi. "The Poor Performance of Students in Community Secondary Schools in Tanzania: A Case of Temeke District." Master of Public Administration Thesis, Mzumbe University, Morogoro Tanzania, 2013.

Ministry of Education, Science and Technology. *Report on Sector Review and Development. Nairobi*: Dar es Salaam: Government Printers, 2003.

MOEST. "Report on Sector Review and Development," 2003.

Momanyi, John Motari, Too, Jackson, and Simiyu, Catherine. "Effect of Students' Age on Academic Motivation and Academic Performance among High School Students in Kenya." *Asian Journal of Education and e-Learning* 3:5 (2015) 337–342.

Mosha, H. J. "Primary Education Policies in Tanzania." *Papers in Education and Development* 16 (1995) 1–16.

Mouton, Johann and Marais, H.C. *Basic Concepts in the Methodology of the Social Sciences.* Pretoria: HSRC Publishers, 1990.

Muhonyiwa, Juliana Masasi. "Factors influencing Poor Examination Performance in Commercial Subjects in Tanzania Ordinary Levels Secondary Schools." Master Thesis in Education Administration, Planning and Policy Studies. Dar es Salaam: The Open University of Tanzania, 2014.

Mligo, Elia Shabani. *Introduction to Research Methods and Report Writing: A Practical Guide to Students and Researchers in Social Science and the Humanities.* Eugene, Oregon: Wipf and Stock/Resource Publications, 2016.

———. *Writing Academic Papers: A Resource Manual for Beginners in Higher-Learning Institutions and Colleges.* Eugene Oregon: Resource Publications/Wipf and Stock, 2012.

Mligo, Elia Shabani and Mwashilindi, Kaombeka Mikael. *English as a Language of Teaching and Learning in Community Secondary Schools in Tanzania: A Critical Analysis.* Eugene, Oregon: Wipf and Stock/Resource, 2017.

Msabila, D.T. and Nalaila, S.G. *Research Proposal and Dissertation Writing: Principle and Practices.* Dar es salaam: Nyambari Nyangwine Publishers, 2013.

Nakalema, Gladys and Ssenyonga, Joseph. "Academic Stress: Its Causes and Results at a Ugandan University." *African Journal of Teacher Education* 3:3 (2013) 1–21.

Ndalichako, Joyce Lazaro. "Examining Classroom Assessment Practices of Secondary School Teachers in Tanzania," (n.d). Online at http://www.iaea.info/documents/paper_226dc3fd1.pdf [Accessed 07 July 2017].

BIBLIOGRAPHY

Ndalichako, J. L. "Towards an Understanding of Assessment Practices of Primary School Teachers in Tanzania. *Zimbabwe Journal of Education Research,*" 16:3 (2004) 168–77. Available online at http://dx.doi.org/10.4314/zjer. v16i3.26046 [Accessed 07 July 2017].

Njabili, Agnes F. *Public Examinations: A Tool for Curriculum Evaluation.* Third Edition. Dar es Salaam: Mture Educational Publishing, 1999.

Neke, Stephen Mueta. "English in Tanzania: An Anatomy of the Hegemony." PhD Thesis, Universiteit Gent, Belgium, 2003.

———. "The Medium of Instruction in Tanzania: Reflections on Language, Education and Secondary Schools in Tanzania." *International Journal of Learning, Teaching and Educational Research* 15 (2016) 117–133.

Neuman, W. Lawrence. *Basics of Social Research: Qualitative and Quantitative Approaches.* Boston, MA.: Pearson Education, 2007.

Nyamubi, Gilman Jackson. "Students' Attitudes and English Language Performance in Secondary Schools in Tanzania." *International Journal of Learning, Teaching and Educational Research* 15 (2016) 117–133.

———. "Determinants of Secondary School Teachers' Job Satisfaction in Tanzania." *Education Research International* (2017) 1–7.

———. "Job Satisfaction as a Determinant of Continuance Commitment among Secondary School Teachers in Tanzania." Journal of Education and Practice 8:22 (2017)

Nyangosia, Patrick Ogecha. "Determinants of Differential Kenya Certificate of Secondary Education Performance and School Effectiveness in Kiambu and Nyeri Counties, Kenya." Master of Education Thesis, Nairobi: Kenyatta University, 2011.

Odumbe, Owino Grace, Simatwa, Enosi M.W. and Oyodo, T.M.O. "Factors Influencing Student Academic Performance in Day-Secondary Schools in Kenya: A Case Study of Migory ub County." *Greener Journal of Educational Research* 5:3 (2015) 78–97.

Ogunniyi, M.B. *Educationaal Measurement and Evaluation.* Ikeja, Lagos State: Longman Nigeria, 1984.

Okumbe, J. A. *Educational Management Theory and Practice.* Nairobi: Nairobi University Press, 2001.

Okumu, I. M., Nakajjo, A. and Isoke, D. *Socio-Economic Determinants of Primary School Dropout: The Logistic Model Analysis.* 2008 Online at http://mpra.ub.uni- muenchen.de/7851/MPRA [Site visited on 17/03/ 2017].

Olalekan, Ajibade Basit. "Influence of Peer Group Relationship on the Academic Performance of Students in Secondary Schools (A Case Study of Selected Secondary Schools in Atiba Local Government Area of Oyo State)." Global Journal of Human-Social: Arts & Humanities–Psychology 16: 4 (2016) 35–47.

Oliver, Paul. *The Student's Guide to Research Ethics.* Philadelphia, PA.: Open University Press, 2003.

BIBLIOGRAPHY

Oluremi, Fareo Dorcas. "Truancy and Academic Performance of Secondary School Students in Southwestern Nigeria: Implications for Counselling." *International Journal for Cross-Disciplinary Subjects in Education* 3:2 (2013) 1424–1428.

Omari, I. M. "Education in Tanzania since Independence." *Papers in Education and Development* 22 (2002) 1–4.

Orodho, J. A. *Techniques of writing Research Proposal and Reports in Educational and Social Sciences: Bureau of Educational Research.* Nairobi: Kenyatta University, 2005.

Orodho, J.A. *Elements of Education and Social Science Research Methods.* Nairobi; Kenya, Kanezja Publisher, 2009.

Owusu-Acheaw, Micheal & Larson, Agatha Gifty. "Reading Habits among Students and its Effect on Academic Performance: A Study of Students of Koforidua Polytechnic" *Library Philosophy and Practice (e-journal).* No.1130, 2014. Online at http://digitalcommons.unl.edu/libphilprac/1130.

Oxford Advanced Learner's Dictionary. Oxford: Oxford University Press, 2010.

Paltridge, Brian and Starfield, Sue. *Thesis and Dissertation Writing in a Second Language: A Handbook for Supervisors.* New York, NY.: Routledge, 2007.

Paul. O. *The Students Guide to Research Ethics.* Philadelphia, PA.: Open University Press, 2003.

Payne, Geoff and Payne, Judy. *Key Concepts in Social Research.* Thousand Oaks, CA.: Sage, 2004.

Pierce, W. David, Cameron, Judy, Banko, Katherine M., and So, Sylvia . "Positive Effects of Rewards and Performance Standards on Intrinsic Motivation." *The Psychological Record* 53 (2003) 561–579.

Projest, Godfrey. "The Effects of Shortage of Teachers on Curriculum Implementation in Community Secondary Schools in Tanzania, The Case of Bukoba Municipality." Master of Education Thesis in Administration, Planning and Policy Studies. The Open University of Tanzania, 2013.

Qorro, Martha. "Language of Instruction in Tanzania: Why Research Findings are not Heeded?" *International Review of Education* 59 (2013) 29–45.

———. "Matatizo ya Kutumia Kiingereza Kufundishia katika Shule za Sekondari na Vyuo vya Juu." *Kioo cha Lugha: Jarida la Kiswahili la Isimu na Fasihi* 3 (2005) 22–30.

———. "Language of Instruction and Its Effects on the Quality of Education." *Papers in Education and Development* 27 (2007) 56–78.

———. "Does Language of Instruction Affect Quality of Education?" *HakiElimu. Working Papers Series.* Dar es Salaam Tanzania, 2006.

Rabin, L.A., Fogel, J. and Nutter-Upham, K.E. Academic Procrastination in College Students: The Role of Self-Reported Executive Function." *Journal of Clinical Experimental Neuropsychology* 33:3 (2011) 344–357.

Reynolds, John Paul. "Factors affecting Academic Procrastination." *Master Theses & Specialist Projects.* Paper 1211, 2015. Online at http://digitalcommons.wku.edu/theses/1511 .

BIBLIOGRAPHY

Schraw, Gregory, Wadkins, Theresa and Olafson, Lori. "Doing the Things We Do: A Grounded Theory of Academic Procrastination." *Journal of Educational Psychology* 99 :1 (2007) 12–25.

Seidman, Irving. *Interviewing as a Qualitative Research: A Guide for Researchers in Education and the Social Sciences*. Third Edition. New York, NY.: Teachers College, University of Columbia, 2006.

Shumox, L. and Lomax, R. "Parental Efficacy: Predictor of Parenting Behaviour and Adolescent Outcomes." *Journal of Parenting* 2 (2001) 127–150.

Singh, Yogesh Kumar. *Fundamentals of Research Methodology and Statistics*. New Delhi: New Age International, 2006.

Skinner, B. F. *The Behavior of Organism: An Experimental Analysis*. New York, NY.: Appleton–Century, 1948.

Solomon, Laura J. and Rothblum, Esther D. "Academic Procrastination: Frequency and Cognitive – Behavioral Correlates." *Journal of Counseling Psychology* 31:4 (1984) 503–509.

Subair, S. Tayo, and Talabi, Rachael Bukola. "Teacher Shortage in Nigerian Schools: Causes, Effects and Administrators Coping Strategies." *Asia Pacific Journal of Education, Arts and Sciences* 2:4 (2015) 31–37.

Suleman, Qaiser, Aslam, Hassan Danial, and Singh, Termit Kaur Ranjit. "Effects of Mild Corporal Punishment on the Academic Achievement of Secondary School Students in Cohat Division, Pakistan." *Research on Humanities and Social Sciences* 4:27 (2014) 56–62.

Temitope, Bankole Emmanuel and Christy, Ogunsakin Funmi. "Influence of Peer-Group on Academic Performance of Secondary School Students in Ekiti State." *International Journal of Innovative Research and Development* 4: 1 (2015) 324–334.

Titiliyo, Musa M. "Absenteeism and Truancy on Academic Performance of Secondary School Students in Ogun State, Nigeria." *Journal of Education and Practice* 5:22 (2014) 81–87.

Tope, Omotere. *Effects of Teachers' Competence on Students' Academic Performance: A Case Study of Ikeja Local Government Area of Lagos State*. Ijebu-Ode, Ogun State Nigeria: EgoBooster Books, 2012. Online at www.omotere.tk [Accessed 31 August, 2017]

Uhrain, Christopher Eric. "Effect of Class Size on Student Achievement in Secondary School." Doctor of Education Dissertation. Walden University, 2016.

URT. *Poverty and Human Development Report*, 2007.

URT. *Tanzania Education and Training Policy*. Ministry of Education and Culture, Dar es Salaam, 1995.

Unity, Oriakhi and Igbudu, Ujiro. "Influence of Gender on Students' Academic Achievement in Government Subject in Public Secondary Schools in Oredo Local Government Area of Edo State, Nigeria." *Journal of Educational and Social Research* 5: 2 (2015) 101–105.

Vandenberg, Kristy Chandler . "Class Size and Academic Achievement." *Electronic Theses & Dissertations*. No.408, 2012. Georgia Southern

BIBLIOGRAPHY

University, Statesboro, Georgia. http://digitalcommons.georgiasouthern.edu/etd/408 [Accessed 31 August 2017].

Voyles, Margaret Jennifer. "Student Academic Success as Related to Student Age and Gender." Doctor of Education Dissertation. The University of Tennessee at Chattanooga Chattanooga, Tennessee, 2011.

Yaghambe, Regina Slaa. "Disciplinary Networks in Secondary Schools: Policy Dimensions and Children's Rights in Tanzania." *Journal of Studies in Education* 3:4 (2013) 43-56

Yahaya, A., Hashim, S., Jamaludin, R. and Kadir, H. "The Effects of Various Modes of Absenteeism Problem in School on the Academic Performance of Students in Secondary Schools." *European Journal of Social Sciences* 12 (2010) 293-298.

Yusuf, Hanna Onyi and Dada, Abdullahi Aliyu. "Impact of Teachers' Qualification and Experience on the Performance of Students in Colleges of Education in Kaduna State, Nigeria." *The Online Journal of Quality in Higher Education* 3:2 (2016) 52-61. Online at www.tojqih.net [Accessed 29 August 2017].

www.ingramcontent.com/pod-product-compliance
Lightning Source LLC
Chambersburg PA
CBHW070501090426
42735CB00012B/2640